Textbooks on Political Analysis

This series introduces a wide array of topics in quantitative methodology for political science and international relations. In recognition of the high demand for quantitative skills in both the applied and academic political fields, *Textbooks on Political Analysis* fills the needs of faculty, students, and independent practitioners as they develop new skills or teach them to others. The books in the series are applied in nature and include exercises at the end of each chapter for readers to complete. Most books in the series focus on how to use software such as R or Stata, though some focus on theory and interpretations associated with methods with real data examples to supplement. Topics covered range widely from introductory undergraduate methods to advanced computational social science. Noteworthy subjects that these books will address include methods of causal inference, best practices for studying international events, ecological inference with electoral applications, survey research methods, and methods in machine learning. Each book contains example data and software code, where appropriate, as supplied by the authors. Ideally, an independent reader should be able to follow the in-text examples without outside help and replicate the author's instruction.

More information about this series at http://www.springer.com/series/15871

Josh Cutler • Matt Dickenson

Computational Frameworks for Political and Social Research with Python

Josh Cutler
Optum Inc.
Minneapolis, MN, USA

Matt Dickenson
Uber Technologies
Denver, CO, USA

ISSN 2522-0373 ISSN 2522-0381 (electronic)
Textbooks on Political Analysis
ISBN 978-3-030-36828-9 ISBN 978-3-030-36826-5 (eBook)
https://doi.org/10.1007/978-3-030-36826-5

© Springer Nature Switzerland AG 2020
This work is subject to copyright. All rights are reserved by the Publisher, whether the whole or part of the material is concerned, specifically the rights of translation, reprinting, reuse of illustrations, recitation, broadcasting, reproduction on microfilms or in any other physical way, and transmission or information storage and retrieval, electronic adaptation, computer software, or by similar or dissimilar methodology now known or hereafter developed.
The use of general descriptive names, registered names, trademarks, service marks, etc. in this publication does not imply, even in the absence of a specific statement, that such names are exempt from the relevant protective laws and regulations and therefore free for general use.
The publisher, the authors, and the editors are safe to assume that the advice and information in this book are believed to be true and accurate at the date of publication. Neither the publisher nor the authors or the editors give a warranty, expressed or implied, with respect to the material contained herein or for any errors or omissions that may have been made. The publisher remains neutral with regard to jurisdictional claims in published maps and institutional affiliations.

This Springer imprint is published by the registered company Springer Nature Switzerland AG
The registered company address is: Gewerbestrasse 11, 6330 Cham, Switzerland

Preface

What Is the Purpose of This Book?

This book introduces concepts from Computer Science and Software Engineering using the Python programming language. The goal is to give readers a strong working knowledge of the skills necessary to use programming in their social science research. We also survey more advanced topics to give readers familiarity with computational modeling and data analysis to serve as a starting point for further learning.

In recent years, knowledge of one or more programming languages has become a valuable part of the social science toolkit. One example is R, which is widely used in both statistics and the social sciences.[1] As social science researchers wish to take on more data-intensive tasks (such as web scraping, machine learning, and image processing), we claim that incorporating Python into their workflow will become an increasingly valuable skill.

Although both R and Python can in theory be used for any programming task, the availability of well-documented and widely supported libraries makes some tasks easier in one ecosystem than another. In Chap. 10 we show how to use the popular Pandas library for data analysis. For image processing, Chap. 13 demonstrates the use of OpenCV and other widely used libraries. Python also offers strong support for natural language processing, as demonstrated in Chap. 14. Readers interested in pursuing other advanced technologies beyond the scope of this text, such as TensorFlow for machine learning and Spark for large-scale distributed computing, will also benefit from a knowledge of Python.

We do not argue in this text that social scientists should not learn R. Rather, we claim that once a researcher is comfortable using R, Python is a compelling choice for the next programming language to learn. It is also a more natural choice for

---

[1] See Monogan, J. E. (2015). Political analysis using R. https://link.springer.com/book/10.1007/978-3-319-23446-5.

illustrating fundamental concepts from computer science and computational social science. The ability to read Python code will also make work in these and other disciplines outside social science more accessible. Throughout this text we will make references to certain syntactic differences between the two languages to help readers familiar with R translate their knowledge to Python.

Who Should Read This Book?

This book is recommended for people with some programming skill but no formal computer science education. We assume that readers are familiar with basic syntax and programming concepts (e.g., looping, conditionals, functions). We will not assume that readers are familiar with big O complexity, data structures, databases, or any other specialized computer science topics.

Familiarity with Python and its concepts (object-oriented programming, OOP) will allow you to hit the ground running. Chapter 1 introduces these topics and provides references for further reading.

Why Write This Book?

This book grew out of a course in the Political Science Department at Duke University. That course was designed to introduce graduate and doctoral students to some of the computational tools that they could use in their research. Initial versions of this course were designed to help social scientists create new and interesting datasets by leveraging the internet and previously ignored unstructured data sources.

How Should I Use This Book?

This book can be used in either of two ways: as a self-teaching tool or as the basis for an advanced undergraduate- or graduate-level course.

Auto-didactic Approach

To get the most out of the book for self-teaching purposes, we recommend starting with the introduction to Python in Chap. 1 and following the references for additional reading until you are comfortable writing and running small Python programs with loops and branching logic. Then read the chapters one at a time (the length should be comfortable for reading each chapter in a single sitting) and look up related material for unfamiliar concepts. We suggest doing all of the homework exercises in the first portion of the book (Chaps. 3 through 10), even if you know conceptually how to perform the same task in a language other than Python. After completing the first section, readers can focus on chapters of interest in the latter section since these chapters do not build upon one another.

Pedagogical Approach

The second way to use this book, and the one that we focused on in writing it, is as the textbook for a one-semester (or one-quarter) course. Students in the course at Duke University were primarily graduate and doctoral students, though some upper-level undergraduates also participated. The modal programming background was familiarity with the R language, and some students also understood the basics of a markup language (e.g., HTML) or another programming language (e.g., Perl).

To use this book for a course, we recommend a one chapter per week schedule. If the term is long enough, extra time can be allotted in the beginning for preparing students' background knowledge or at the end for special topics and final projects. We have taught the course with once-a-week (3 h) or twice-a-week meetings (1.5 h each) and prefer the latter schedule. The first class meeting of the week is used to introduce the conceptual material and provide demonstrations, and the second meeting is used as an interactive lab session. There should be enough time between the second meeting of 1 week and the first meeting of the next week for students to complete the homework assignment.

The course then concludes with presentation of student projects. This book is structured so that the material will be cumulative and by the end of the semester students will have the tools to create a program that is useful for social science research. The exact form of the final project is very flexible, but it should be a nontrivial application of what has been covered and result in a library or tool that can be used for research after the course is over. Examples of feasible projects include:

1. A library that queries Twitter's API, stores tweets, and classifies them according to their sentiment
2. A library that allows you to scrape websites of interest and extract keywords to aid in human moderated coding
3. An agent-based model o f asocial problem

Lab Sessions

Most lab sessions will start in the same way: with a short script of starter code and a set of instructions. The instructions will specify parts of the starter code that are broken and need to be fixed, and/or functions and commands that should be added to the code in order to make it run properly. Later in the book the lab instructions will be at a more conceptual level and require participants to work out the implementation details themselves.

Each lab is meant to fill about 1–1.5 h. However, do not worry if there is not enough time to complete all of the material. Often the basic idea of the lab can be grasped in the first few exercises, and the later ones build on this. If desired, unfinished portions of the lab can be assigned in addition to the homework. After a lecture on the concepts discussed in the chapter and completion of the lab exercises, students should be prepared to complete the homework.

If the material in the preceding chapter is not sufficient to solve the challenges in lab, participants are encouraged to find online resources to bridge the gap. This process of finding documentation online is a prominent part of most programmers' workflow, and students should not be embarrassed about doing so. Note that this is quite different from trying to find exact solutions that can be copied and pasted.

Data

Several examples in this book will refer to data that we have made available on the Harvard Dataverse. The dataverse for this book can be found at https://dataverse.harvard.edu/dataverse/python-book. Within that dataverse, we plan to release one dataset corresponding to each edition of this text. The persistent link for the data used in the present edition is https://dataverse.harvard.edu/dataset.xhtml?persistentId=doi:10.7910/DVN/MLOQ21.

Website and Errata

Software environments, libraries, and best practices change at a relatively quick pace. To keep up with these developments, we offer a website to accompany this book at https://computational-frameworks-python-book.github.io/. The website will be updated with errata as we become aware of them. If there are significant changes to any of the packages used in the book that impact their suitability for teaching or research, we will make those announcements on the site as well.

Structure of the Book

The first section of the book (Chaps. 3 through 9) is devoted to making sure that the reader is comfortable with building simple, object-oriented programs. We cover best practices in software engineering as well as basic computer science concepts, data structures, algorithm design, and computational complexity. Homeworks in this section are designed to familiarize the reader with implementing simple programs.

The latter half of the book (Chap. 10 onward) is devoted to applying computational tools to the field of social science. We cover some specific programming techniques that are of use to social scientists (e.g., classification, linear programming) and implement some simple examples of these. If the book is used as a course outline, this section can also be used for further exploration of specific topics and for student projects.

Acknowledgments

The material presented here was first taught as a graduate-level Python course in the Duke University Department of Political Science in 2012 and 2013. Both authors are grateful for the support they received from the department to work on this course, especially from Michael D. Ward and Scott de Marchi. Participants in these early iterations of the course provided a testing ground for the ideas presented here, and we appreciate their feedback.

A subsequent version was offered as a short course at Washington University in St. Louis in 2014 under the supervision of Jacob Montgomery. We are particularly grateful to David Carlson, Michelle Torres, and Erin Rossiter for providing ongoing feedback on the application of this material to political science research.

We also appreciate the feedback we have received from our editor, James E. Monogan III, and reviewers including Florian Hollenbach and Shahryar Minhas. Lorraine Klimowich, Kelly Daugherty, and Faith Su at Springer have been helpful at every turn.

We sincerely hope that this book helps to improve the capabilities of political and social researchers. Any errors in the text remain our responsibility alone.

Minneapolis, MN, USA Josh Cutler
Denver, CO, USA Matt Dickenson
April 2018

Contents

Part I Python for Data Collection and Analysis

1 Getting Started with Python 3
   1.1   Overview 3
   1.2   Background 3
          1.2.1   Python 2 and 3 4
          1.2.2   Installation 4
          1.2.3   Anaconda 5
          1.2.4   Shells 6
          1.2.5   Dependencies 7
          1.2.6   The Significance of Whitespace 7
   1.3   Data Types 9
          1.3.1   Integers 9
          1.3.2   Floating-Point Numbers 11
          1.3.3   Strings 12
          1.3.4   Boolean Values 12
   1.4   Functions 13
   1.5   Collections 15
          1.5.1   Lists 15
          1.5.2   Loops 17
          1.5.3   Dictionaries 18
   1.6   Conclusion 19
   Reference 19

2 Building Software 21
   2.1   The Software World 21
          2.1.1   A Powerful Ecosystem 21
          2.1.2   Collaboration Across Time and Space 22
   2.2   Source Control 22
          2.2.1   Getting Started with Git 23
   2.3   Lab Session 29
   References 32

3	**Object-Oriented Programming**			33
	3.1	Object-Oriented Design		34
		3.1.1	Objects, Classes, and Instances	34
		3.1.2	Example: Fibonacci Numbers	35
		3.1.3	Inheritance and Polymorphism	37
		3.1.4	Design Choices	39
	3.2	Why OOP?		40
	3.3	Lab Session		41
		3.3.1	Review: Python Functions and Magic Methods	41
		3.3.2	Example: The Median Voter Theorem	42
	References			48
4	**Introduction to Algorithms**			49
	4.1	Algorithms		49
		4.1.1	Sorting	50
		4.1.2	Computational Complexity	50
		4.1.3	Selection Sort	53
		4.1.4	Merge Sort	53
		4.1.5	The Economics of Algorithms	54
	4.2	Going Deeper		54
	4.3	Lab Session		55
		4.3.1	Group Exercise	55
		4.3.2	Lab Practice	56
	References			57
5	**Introduction to Data Structures**			59
	5.1	Arrays and Lists		60
	5.2	Queues and Stacks		61
	5.3	Dictionaries and Hashtables		63
	5.4	Trees and Heaps		63
	5.5	Graphs		65
	5.6	Lab Session		66
	Reference			71
6	**Input, Output, and the Web**			73
	6.1	Disks		73
	6.2	The Cost of Input and Output		74
	6.3	Writing to the Disk in Python		74
		6.3.1	CSV Files	77
	6.4	HTML and HTTP		78
	6.5	Lab Session		81
		6.5.1	Regular Expressions	81
		6.5.2	Web Scraping	83
	Reference			85

Contents

7   Application Programming Interfaces 87
  7.1   Application Programming Interfaces (APIs) 88
  7.2   REST Is Good 89
  7.3   More on HTML and HTTP 89
  7.4   CRUD 91
  7.5   The Twitter API 91
  7.6   Lab Session 93
    7.6.1   Huffington Post 93
    7.6.2   Google 95
  References 97

8   Databases 99
  8.1   Types of Databases 99
  8.2   Why SQL? 100
  8.3   Schemas 102
  8.4   Queries 103
  8.5   Object Relational Mapping (ORM) 105
  8.6   In-Class Example 106
  8.7   Lab Session 111

9   NoSQL Databases 117
  9.1   Why NoSQL? 118
  9.2   How Does NoSQL Work? 118
  9.3   In-Class Example 119
  9.4   Lab Session 123

Part II   Advanced Topics

10   Introduction to Machine Learning with Python 129
  10.1   Bayes' Rule: Review and Example 130
  10.2   Metrics: Precision and Recall 131
  10.3   LaPlacean Smoothing 132
  10.4   Implementing a Classifier 133
  10.5   Lab Session 137
    10.5.1   Series 138
    10.5.2   DataFrames 140
  10.6   Linear Modeling 141
  10.7   Plotting 141
  10.8   Further Reading 142

11   Linear Programming 143
  11.1   PuLP 144
  11.2   Example: Paintings 144
  11.3   Example: Airlines 146
  11.4   Set Partitioning 147
  11.5   Feasibility 149
  References 149

12	**Practical Programming**		151
	12.1	Exceptions	151
	12.2	Testing	155
		12.2.1 Motivation for Testing	155
		12.2.2 Practicing Unit Tests	156
	12.3	Lab Session	158
		12.3.1 Starter Code	158
		12.3.2 Tests	160
13	**Case Study: Image Processing**		165
	13.1	Working with Image Data	166
		13.1.1 Data Formats	167
		13.1.2 Reading Images in Python	169
		13.1.3 Feature Extraction	171
	13.2	Nighttime Lights and Population	173
		13.2.1 Nighttime Lights Data	173
		13.2.2 Population Estimates	174
		13.2.3 Code Walk-through	175
		13.2.4 Results	187
	13.3	Additional Applications and Further Reading	187
	References		188
14	**Case Study: Natural Language Processing**		191
	14.1	Working with Text Data	191
		14.1.1 Text as Data	192
		14.1.2 Transformation	195
	14.2	Party and Social Media	196
		14.2.1 US Senators' Tweets	197
		14.2.2 Tweet Normalization	199
		14.2.3 EDA	200
		14.2.4 Results	202
	14.3	Additional Applications and Further Reading	203
	References		204
15	**Conclusion**		205
	15.1	Next Steps	206
	15.2	Closing	207
Index			209

Acronyms

API   Application Programming Interface: a defined structure for interacting with an external program, service, or data source.
CSV   Comma-Separated Values: a comma-delimited flat file format for data storage.
HTML   HyperText Markup Language: a markup language for encoding documents that is both human and machine readable and supports multimedia.
HTTP   Hypertext Transfer Protocol: the foundation of data communication for the World Wide Web.
JSON   JavaScript Object Notation: a human-readable data format primarily used in JavaScript but supported in many popular programming languages.
ORM   Object Relational Mapping: a tool for converting data between its stored representation in a database and its in-memory representation as a Python object.
REST   Representational State Transfer: an architectural design for programming interfaces that identify and transmit resources.
SQL   Structured Query Language: a domain-specific language for interacting with databases.
XML   Extensible Markup Language: a markup language for encoding documents that is both human and machine readable, similar to HTML.

Part I
Python for Data Collection and Analysis

The following chapters constitute the core portion of the book. They introduce the Python programming language and demonstrate its use for data collection and analysis. The material in these chapters is meant to be covered in sequence. We recommend that you read through the chapters in order and work through the homework and lab sessions before moving on to the material in Part II.

Chapter 1
Getting Started with Python

1.1 Overview

This chapter introduces basic Python concepts that will be used throughout the remainder of this text. If you are already familiar with another programming language, such as R, many of the concepts here will be analogous. If you are approaching Python as your first programming language (and it is a good choice for that purpose), you may benefit from working through this material alongside another introductory text such as [1].

1.2 Background

Python was originally released in 1991, but its popularity greatly increased after the release of version 2.0 of the language in 2000. Common use cases for the language include scientific computing, data analysis, and web development. Although the language is now well into 3× versions, many useful libraries were created for (and still support) Python 2, so the most recent version of Python 2 (2.7) remains very popular although it will not receive any long-term support from the language maintainers after January 1, 2020.

In this book we focus on Python 3, but most of the code in this book could be converted to Python 2 with minimal effort if needed. At this point you do not need to worry about the difference between these versions of Python, but it is something to be aware of going forward. To minimize headaches as you work through the book, pick a version and stick with it throughout the exercises.

1.2.1 Python 2 and 3

If you do choose to work with Python 2 (or find yourself needing to convert code written in Python 2 to Python 3 or vice versa), there are three significant differences to be aware of. They are changes to the behavior of the division operator and the print function, and support for Unicode strings. If you are not familiar with these now, feel free to return to this section after completing the first section of the book.

In Python 2 the division operator behaves as floor division ("rounding down") when used with integers. For example, `8 / 5` returns `1` and `-8 / 5` returns `-2`. If either the numerator or the divisor (or both) are floating-point numbers, you will get a float as the return value. In Python 3 on the other hand, division with integers will always result in a float. (`8 / 5` results in `1.6` and `-8 / 5` results in `-1.6`). We find that the latter behavior is often more intuitive for beginners.

You can see another difference in how the **print** function is called. In Python 2 you can use **print** with or without parentheses: **print** `"hello world"` and **print**`("hello world")` are perfectly equivalent. Python 3 requires parentheses, so only **print**`("hello world")` will work. This difference is one way to tell whether code you find online is intended for use with Python 2 or 3, but of course you can choose to use parentheses in either case.

The third major difference is in how Unicode strings are handled. Python 2 treats Unicode strings as a different type from regular strings. You can see this by checking **type**`('hello world regular')` and **type**`(u'hello world unicode')` (note the presence of a u preceding the string). In Python 2 the first will return `<`**type** `'str'>` and the second will return `<`**type** `'unicode'>`. In Python 3 both results will be `<`**type** `'str'>`. Unicode support is one advantage of Python 3 over Python 2, especially when using text data from sources such as the web and Twitter. We will show several examples of this in later chapters, particularly when dealing with text on the web. For most of the code in this book you can safely address these differences with minimal conversion if you choose to use Python 2 instead.

1.2.2 Installation

Python's popularity is so great that there is a good chance that it is already installed on your computer. One way to verify this is to open your terminal program (Terminal on MacOS or the "Command prompt window" on Windows), type `python`, and hit Enter.

If you see something like the following on MacOS:

```
Python 3.7.3 (default, Jun 19 2019, 07:40:11)
[Clang 9.0.0 (clang-900.0.39.2)] on darwin
Type "help", "copyright", "credits" or "license" for
    more information.
```

1.2 Background

```
>>>
```

or this on Windows:

```
Python 3.7.3 (default, Jun 19 2019, 07:40:11) [MSC
    v.1500 32 bit (Intel)] on win32
Type "help", "copyright", "credits" or "license" for
    more information.
>>>
```

then Python is already installed and ready to use.

If you see an error message (`command not found: python`), this means that Python is not installed on your computer. Follow the instructions at https://docs.python.org/2/using/index.html for your system and ensure that the example above works when you are done, or follow the instructions for using Anaconda recommended in the next section.

We will use the convention `>>>` as the preface for code you are expected to input interactively in the Python console. When you see lines prefaced by `>>>` intermingled with lines that do not have that prefix, the latter lines are illustrating the expected output of your code. In later chapters you will see code prefaced with line numbers. This code will work when typed into the console interactively, but we recommend saving it in a text file with a `.py` extension instead. You can then run this code from the command line or interactively by copying it and pasting it into the Python console. Note that the significance of whitespace in Python, which we discuss in more detail below, means that you can only copy and paste one "block" of code at a time: blank lines in a function or class definition will prevent you from being able to copy-paste. For code that is more than a few lines (such as a single function), we recommend writing it in a Python text file and running it from the command line with a command such as `python my_file.py`.

1.2.3 Anaconda

For beginners or anyone having difficulty setting up and managing their Python environment, we recommend looking at Anaconda. Anaconda is an *environment manager* that makes it easier to work on multiple Python projects with different dependencies (including different versions of the Python language itself, if you wish) on a single computer.

To install Anaconda, visit https://www.anaconda.org. Choose the latest Python version (or any version you prefer, if you have a reason for choosing another one), which at the time of this writing is "Python 3.7 version." Follow the installation instructions presented there. If you need more help, documentation can be found at https://docs.conda.io/projects/conda/en/latest/user-guide/getting-started.html.

After installing Anaconda, start a new terminal session (a new tab or window in your terminal application). You should see your command prompt prefaced by the name of the Anaconda environment you are using, which is `base` by default. Check the Anaconda version by running `conda --version` and ensure that it does not return an error (for example, you might see `conda 4.6.11`). Check the Python version with `python --version` and sure that it matches the value you were expecting (e.g., `Python 3.7.3`).

One thing to note about Anaconda is that it is a powerful tool and includes many features that we do not reference in this text. For example, you can also use Anaconda to manage projects in other programming languages such as C and R. You can also use Anaconda as a package manager (`conda install ...`). However, in this text we use Pip as the package manager and Anaconda only as an environment manager. This is because Pip remains the more standard package manager for Python, and knowledge of it is transferrable even to programming environments that are not managed by Anaconda.

As the Python ecosystem is always changing, reference this book's website at https://computational-frameworks-python-book.github.io/ for the latest updates on setting up your environment.

1.2.4 Shells

One idea that often confuses Python beginners is the difference between their operating system command line (or "shell") and using Python interactively. In both cases you are interactively sending commands to your computer and seeing the results immediately—the difference is in how the commands will be interpreted. The Python interpreter is trying to run the commands that you send as if they are Python, whereas the system command line will be running them as if they are system commands.

In this book we will follow the convention of prefixing shell commands with `$` and interactive Python commands with `>>>`. This follows the default command-line prompt in each of these environments.

For example, when you open your operating system's terminal, you can type commands like the following:

`$ echo hello world`

To do the equivalent in Python 3, the command is

`>>> print("hello world")`

When you are using your terminal and wish to open Python, the command is

`$ python`

and then you will see the command prompt change to `>>>`. If you are using Python and need to quit in order to perform a terminal command, use the `exit()` command. Then you will see your command prompt change from `>>>` to `$` because you have exited Python and are back to the command prompt in your terminal application.

We will use the convention $ to indicate lines that you are expected to run in your computer's shell (rather than in the Python console). There will be very few of these, and they will mostly involve installing packages that our code depends on as discussed in the next section.

1.2.5 Dependencies

One reason to learn Python is to be able to make use of all the software that other developers have written for the language. In order to do this, you need to be able to install the software that they have written. Python comes with a built-in tool for installing dependencies, called `pip`.[1] You run `pip` in your terminal (not inside of an interactive Python environment). For example, if we wanted to install the `requests` library the command would be

```
$ pip install requests
```

Whenever you need to install dependencies in order to use the code in this book we will provide the specific installation command to run.

1.2.6 The Significance of Whitespace

One major syntactic difference between Python and other programming languages is the way that it treats whitespace. Whitespace in Python is *syntactically significant*, meaning that consistent indentation (and to a certain extent, the role of blank lines) is enforced by the language.

To see this error in action, try adding unneeded whitespace at the beginning of a line and you will see an error like the following:

```
>>>    x = 42
  File "<stdin>", line 1
    x = 42
    ^
IndentationError: unexpected indent
```

This type of consistency enforcement is one of the things that helps with readability of Python code. It also means that Python code (at least in this respect) tends to be stylistically similar across projects.

However, this does force you to do a few things differently as a developer compared to working in other languages. First, choose the type and amount of

---

[1] This is true for Python versions 2.7.9 and after. If you do not have `pip` installed, see https://pip.pypa.io/en/stable/installing/.

indentation you will use. We recommend four spaces, as this is the most common style for Python. This means that your outermost code will not be indented at all, the first level of indentation (such as inside a function definition) will be indented four spaces, the next level eight spaces, and so on. Another popular choice is two spaces. We do not recommend the use of tabs for indentation since tabs behave differently on different platforms (e.g., Windows vs. Unix), and choosing odd numbers for indentation is generally considered to be undesirable.

The second thing to be aware of is that whatever amount and type of styling you choose, you must be consistent. Within a single Python file this will be enforced by the language itself at runtime, and across files within a project it is beneficial to maintain consistency for readability and to reduce cognitive overhead as you switch between different files. Almost all text editors that you will use allow you to set up shortcuts to specify the amount of whitespace you want to use in a project, so that the "Tab" key becomes a shortcut for that number of spaces.

You must also be consistent with your use of whitespace within an interactive Python session. For example, when writing an **if** clause, we cannot change our amount of indentation to four spaces if we started with two on the first line (the amount of indentation is inferred by the interpreter from the first indented line):

```
>>> if x == 7:
...   print("hello")
...       print("goodbye")
  File "<stdin>", line 3
    print("goodbye")
    ^
IndentationError: unexpected indent
```

Finally, you should understand that this also impacts your ability to define functions in the interactive console. When defining functions in text files it is generally good style to leave blank lines between different parts of the code to help with readability. However, in the Python console a blank line is taken to indicate the end of a function. This means that if you define functions interactively—or even copy and paste them from files—you must remove any blank lines to prevent errors.

We can encounter a simple example of this problem by copying and pasting the following function into a Python console:

```
1  def foo():
2      print("hello")
3
4      print("goodbye")
```

The error we will see is as follows:

```
>>> def foo():
...     print("hello")
...
>>>     print("goodbye")
```

```
File "<stdin>", line 1
    print("goodbye")
    ^
IndentationError: unexpected indent
```

Because we included a blank line, the Python interpreter inferred that our function ended after `print("hello")` and so when it encountered the line `print("goodbye")` it no longer had the context to know that we were still in the process of defining our function.

These whitespace rules can be somewhat tricky at first, especially if you are coming from working in a language that does not enforce similar rules. If you remember two simple rules—to be consistent with your indentation, and to skip blank lines when working with indented blocks in the console—you will quickly become accustomed to this feature of Python.

1.3 Data Types

This section introduces the most widely used native data types in Python. You will find yourself using these types over and over again, so it is worth understanding the differences between them and when the usage of each is appropriate.

1.3.1 Integers

Once you open the Python interpreter, you might be wondering what you can do next.[2] Perhaps the simplest thing you can do (besides printing a phrase as we did above) is to use it as a calculator. Table 1.1 lists the operations available to you and their names.

Table 1.1 Common mathematical operators

Operator	Name
=	Assignment
+	Addition
-	Subtraction
*	Multiplication
/	Division
**	Exponent
%	Modulus

---

[2] Also known as a REPL, which stands for "read, evaluate, print loop." This describes exactly what happens: the interpreter reads your input, evaluates it, and prints the output.

The first six are quite straightforward:

```
>>> x = 5 # assignment
>>> 1 + 2 # addition
>>> 6 * 7 # multiplication
>>> 5 - 3 # subtraction
>>> 15 / 3 # division
>>> 2 ** 3 # exponentiation
```

If you enter these one line at a time, you will see output for each. If you copy and paste them as a block of 6 commands, you will only see output for the final line. If you want to be able to both copy-paste the commands into the interactive terminal and ensure that output is displayed for each, wrap each command in a `print()` function. For example, `print(15/3)` will print `5.0`. Note that you should exclude the comment at the end of the line from the body of your print function, since it will cause the closing paren to also be commented-out.

The # character indicates a comment. You can include these in the code that you type interactively, but you do not have to. Code on a line after a # is ignored by the Python interpreter. It is intended mostly to provide contextual information to human readers of your code, and is more useful when typing code in a file that will be saved. If you have code in a file that you do not wish to run, you can also "comment out" the code by prefacing one or more lines with comment characters. Many text editors have shortcuts for doing this: search the help menu of your favorite editor to see if this is available.

The modulo operator might be new to you. To see its value, look at an example of division with a remainder:

```
>>> 17 / 3
```

What does this evaluate to and does that match what you expect? In Python 3 this will return the answer `5.666666666666667`. However, if we want the result of integer division (only the whole number result, not the fraction), we can use `17 // 3` instead. This returns 5.[3]

If we wanted to get the remainder of this operation, that is where the modulo operator comes in:

```
>>> 17 % 3
```

To get both the quotient and the remainder in integer division, we have to perform two operations:

```
>>> numerator = 17
>>> denominator = 3
>>> quotient = numerator // denominator
>>> remainder = numerator % denominator
```

---

[3] Python 2 used integer division by default, so `17 / 3` would return 5.

1.3 Data Types

Here we are using the assignment operator = to set the value of variables named numerator and denominator. Then we assign the result of division to a variable called quotient and the result of the modulo operation to remainder. There is nothing special about these variable names, they just happen to be descriptive of the values that they represent. To view the results, you can either type quotient by itself on a line (and hit return) or **print**(quotient). The same applies for the remainder variable.

We already mentioned that whole numbers are called integers, and that is the name of their Python data type. What about when we work with fractional numbers, such as 5.666? For that, we will need floating-point numbers.

1.3.2 Floating-Point Numbers

Floating-point numbers (or "float" for short) allow us to work with decimals. To work through the same division problem with floating-point numbers, try the following:

```
>>> 17.0 / 3.0
```

Since both the numerator and denominator are floating-point numbers, the result we get back is also a float. Actually, Python will return a floating-point number if *either* the numerator or denominator is a float:

```
>>> 17.0 / 3
>>> 17 / 3.0
```

How can you tell in a programmatic fashion whether the number you are dealing with is a float or an integer? One way is with the **type** function, which will tell you the type of any Python object:

```
>>> type(42)
<type 'int'>
>>> type(42.0)
<type 'float'>
```

These short names for the data types also tell you how to convert between types. To turn a float into an integer, use the **int** function and to do the reverse use the **float** function:

```
>>> int(42.0)
>>> float(42)
```

What happens if you use the **int** function on a floating point that has a non-zero decimal value?

```
>>> int(42.5)
42
```

This is essentially the same behavior we saw above with our `17 // 3` example: the extra precision is lost.

Note that you may sometimes see floats written with a decimal point but no decimal value specified, e.g.:

```
>>> 3. / 2
1.5
```

This is treated exactly as if you had written:

```
>>> 3.0 / 2
1.5
```

1.3.3 Strings

What about non-numeric data types? The most common of these, sequences of characters, is called a string. Unlike some other languages, there is no separate type in Python for individual characters: "a" or "b" are simply strings of length one.

You have already encountered strings in the example above where we printed `"hello world"`.[4] Some of the mathematical operations we have been using also work with strings:

```
>>> "hello" + "world"
'helloworld'
```

Notice that there is nothing special about strings that contain words, so Python does not add a space between them; if we wanted the input to be human readable, we would have to put a space into either the end of the first string or the beginning of the second one. (We could also use another function that we will see a bit later, but that requires another data type that we have not yet introduced.)

Similarly, you can also multiply strings:

```
>>> "hello" * 3
'hellohellohello'
```

Note that this will *not* work if the numeric value is a float, since the idea of a "partial" string is undefined. Similarly, subtraction, division, and exponentiation of strings are all undefined.

1.3.4 Boolean Values

One nice behavior that *is* defined for strings is the notion of containment, i.e. whether one string contains the other.

---

[4] Unlike some other languages, there is no difference in Python between double-quoted and single-quoted strings. The only requirement is that they match, i.e. `"hello'` is invalid.

```
>>> "world" in "hello world"
True
```

The value that this evaluates to—True—is a value that we have not encountered before: a Boolean (or "bool"). The two available Boolean values are True and False. These are also the values returned when we check the equality of two numbers. Try the following to see which are true and which are false:

```
>>> 1 == 1
>>> 1 == 2
>>> 1 == 1.0
>>> 1 == '1'
>>> 1 < 2
>>> 1 > 2
>>> 1 <= 2
>>> 1 >= 2
```

Notice the difference between checking equality (two equals signs, ==) and assigning a value (one equals sign, x = 42). The first is used to compare two values, the latter to set a variable equal to a particular value.

Boolean values can be combined using the logical operators **and** and **or**:

```
>>> True and True
>>> True and False
>>> False and False
>>> True or False
```

It is important to understand the results of these logical combinations, since they are fundamental to programming. Clauses combined with **and** evaluate to true if *both* clauses are true while clauses combined with **or** evaluate to true if *either* sub-clause is true.

We can also combine these operations without setting the results to intermediate variables:

```
>>> (1 == 1) and (1 == 2)
>>> (1 == 1) or (1 == 2)
```

1.4 Functions

Now that you know how to assign values to variables and combine different operations, you are ready to begin defining your own functions. Here is a trivial example:

```
>>> def my_function():
>>>     print("hello world")
```

After defining the function you will need to hit enter twice. This tells the Python interpreter that you are finished defining the function, but does not run it. To run the function, use its name followed by parentheses: `my_function()`. You should see `hello world` in the output.

The **def** keyword indicates that we are defining a function. The next part is the name of the function—the name is entirely up to you, the only conditions are that it must not contain whitespace characters (it must be "one word") and it cannot begin with a numeric character. By convention, Python functions are lowercase and use underscores in place of whitespace (this style is known as "snake case" in contrast to other styles such as "camel case" which is used for class names).

We follow the name with parentheses and a colon to indicate that the next line will contain the function definition. If the function accepted arguments they would be named within the parentheses, but this one does not take any arguments. That means that the behavior of the function is always the same; the caller has no control over what gets displayed. As we discussed above, remember that the whitespace on the next line is important: the body of the function *must* be indented, and it must be indented consistently.

Now let us write a function that takes an argument:

```
>>> def show_word(word):
>>>     print("hello " + word)
```

This function takes an argument called `word`. Notice that we expect this value to be a string (since we are adding it to the string "hello"), but our code does not enforce this at all. To call a function with arguments, use its name and put any arguments inside the parentheses, such as `show_word("Elmo")`. If we had a function that took multiple arguments we would call it by separating the arguments with commas, such as `another_function(1, 2, 3)`.

In Python, you do not need to define the types of data that your function accepts at the time that you define the function. However, if your code depends on data being a certain type in order to work, you have a couple of options available to you. The first is to use the `assert` keyword to make an assertion about the type. Another option is to coerce the data into being the type that you expect. Since every object in Python *should* be able to represent itself as a string, that is the better option in this case.

```
>>> def show_word_safer(word):
>>>     print("hello " + str(word))
```

Again, we can call this function using `show_word_safer("Garfield")`. Notice the difference: instead of assuming that the `word` value is a string, we are using its string value directly. Note that this does not change the value of the argument that is passed anywhere other than inside the function:

```
>>> num = 3
>>> show_word_safer(num)
>>> type(num)
<type 'int'>
```

If we want to be able to affect the type or value of variables outside the scope of a function, we must **return** output:

1.5 Collections

```
def double(number):
    return number * 2
```

Now instead of simply displaying output, we are performing a computation and giving the output back to the caller.

```
>>> num = 3
>>> doubled = double(num)
>>> print(num)  #=> 3
>>> print(doubled)  #=> 6
```

If we want to change the original value, we can use the same variable name for the result of the function:

```
>>> num = 3
>>> num = double(num)
>>> print(num)  #=> 6
```

The flexibility of types can also be an advantage: this function will work for any data type for which multiplication is defined. Recall that this includes strings:

```
>>> val = "hello"
>>> print(double(val))
'hellohello'
```

1.5 Collections

So far the only type of collection we have seen is a string. This is rather limiting, since if we wanted a collection of numeric information it would be impossible to know whether the string "10" represented two values (one and then zero) or one (ten). When we want to combine separate values into a single collection, we need additional types. The most common collection type in Python is a list.

1.5.1 Lists

The most common collection type in Python is a list. The notation for a list is square brackets ([]) with values separated by commas. Unlike some other languages, values of different types can be combined into a single list:

```
>>> my_first_list = [1, "a", 42.0]
```

We can easily convert strings into lists by splitting them on a particular character:

```
>>> "abc def ghi".split(" ")
['abc', 'def', 'ghi']
```

We can also perform the reverse operation. (This is the simpler way to join the strings "hello" and "world" that we alluded to earlier.) We provide a list of strings along with the string that we wish to use to join them together:

```
>>> " ".join(["hello", "world"])
'hello world'
```

Like strings, we can also check whether a list contains a particular value:

```
>>> my_list = [1, 2, 3]
>>> 3 in my_list
True
```

If we want to check the length of a list, we use the **len** function:

```
>>> my_list = [1, 2, 3]
>>> len(my_list)
3
```

If we want to retrieve a specific value, we use its *index*. The first element of the list is available at index 0, the second at index 1, and so on. Note that if you are accustomed to the R language, this is a significant difference since R indexes lists starting at 1.

```
>>> my_list = ["a", "b", "c"]
>>> my_list[0]  #=> "a"
>>> my_list[1]  #=> "b"
>>> my_list[2]  #=> "c"
```

Another way to get the last element of a list would be to check its length and subtract one (to account for the zero-based indexing):

```
>>> my_list[len(my_list)-1]  #=> "c"
```

In fact, the need to access the last element of a list is so common that Python provides a shorthand for this: we can just use -1 without computing the length:

```
>>> my_list[-1]  #=> "c"
```

We can also retrieve elements in sequence:

```
>>> my_list = ["a", "b", "c", "d", "e"]
>>> my_list[2:4]
['c', 'd']
```

The range here is "half-open," meaning that the first index (2 in this case) is *inclusive* but the last index (4) is *exclusive*. So the range 2 : 4 returns the elements at indices 2 and 3, but not 4. Another way to think about this is that my_list[x:y] will return y-x elements, assuming that both are valid, positive indices for the list and do not extend beyond its endpoints.

Notice that if you wanted to retrieve a sub-sequence of a string you could split it into characters and then join them back together. This would be overkill, though, since the same behavior works on strings directly:

1.5 Collections

```
>>> my_string = "abcde"
>>> my_string[2:4]
'cd'
```

Lists are a powerful tool when dealing with collections of data, and they become even more powerful when you understand how to work with loops.

1.5.2 Loops

1.5.2.1 For-Loops

The simplest type of loop is one in which we wish to visit every element of a list. This is known as a *for loop* and we can write one in Python like this:

```
>>> my_list = [1, 2, 3]
>>> for x in my_list:
...     print(x)
```

As with defining functions, you will need to hit "Return" twice to get the code to run. This indicates to the Python interpreter that you are done defining the indented block inside the loop. The `for ... in` syntax defines the loop. We specify the list we are iterating over and create the intermediate variable x to refer to each element as we visit it. This is equivalent to doing:

```
>>> print my_list[0]
>>> print my_list[1]
>>> print my_list[2]
```

What are the advantages of using a for-loop instead of operating on each element of the list individually? First, it reduces the repetitiveness of our code. Second, it prevents us from having to check how many elements are in the list: we do the same thing to every element no matter if the list is empty or contains 1000 elements.

1.5.2.2 While-Loops

Another type of loop, known as a while loop, is used to perform an operation as long as a certain condition holds true. We set the initial value of the condition outside the loop, and then iterate until it becomes false.

For example, suppose we want to perform some operation incrementally up to a certain upper bound:

```
>>> count = 0
>>> while (count < 4):
>>>     print('The count is: ', count)
...     count = count + 1
```

Notice that it is possible (accidentally or on purpose) to create *infinite* while loops—loops that have no end. Be very careful with while loops in your code to avoid accidentally setting up loops that never terminate.

1.5.3 Dictionaries

As we have seen, lists are quite useful. You can even have lists of lists. For example, suppose you want to represent the names and ages of a group of people. You could set up each person's data as its own list, and then group all of these together in a larger list. However, you would have to set up some convention such as remembering that the name always came first and the age second or vice versa.

If you find yourself setting up lists where the placement of a value is semantically meaningful, you might want to use a dictionary instead. Dictionaries allow for quick look-ups of values using *keys* instead of indices. Instead of remembering that "name" is at index 0 and "age" is at index 1, you could set these strings up as keys directly:

```
>>> person_dictionary = {"name": "Mary", "age": 99}
>>> person_dictionary["name"] #=> "Mary"
>>> person_dictionary["age"] #=> 99
```

You can also loop over dictionaries using its keys, its values, or both:

```
1  >>> for k in person_dictionary.keys():
2  ...      print(k)
3  ...
4  age
5  name
6  >>> for v in person_dictionary.values():
7  ...  print(v)
8  ...
9  99
10 Mary
11 >>> for k, v in person_dictionary.items():
12 ...  print("key " + k + " is " + str(v))
13 ...
14 key age is 99
15 key name is Mary
```

Dictionaries make it easy to refer to your values with meaningful names, rather than remembering list indices.[5] They also form the basis of many other data structures that we will use in later chapters.

---

[5] Note that if you are using Python 2 instead of 3, the last example above should use `person_dictionary.iteritems()` instead of `person_dictionary.items()`.

1.6 Conclusion

This chapter introduced the most basic components of Python: individual values, collections, and functions. These will be used in every subsequent chapter, so practice with these concepts until you feel comfortable using them.

Reference

1. Shaw, Z. (2013). *Learn python the hard way.* Retrieved March 24, 2018, from https://learnpythonthehardway.org/book/

Chapter 2
Building Software

Software development is a social process. Although this book does not attempt to develop a detailed social theory of the work that goes into creating software, we expect that a brief sketch of the means by which teams of developers collaborate across time and space will be valuable to our readers. This chapter introduces the concepts of version control, a powerful tool that facilitates the long-term success of software projects.

2.1 The Software World

2.1.1 A Powerful Ecosystem

Ultimately all software is developed by and for humans, and thus cannot be separated from the social realm. The popular image of a single coder working on a project alone in the dark of night is only possible because the progress of software tools has enabled individual developers to achieve a level of productivity many orders of magnitude higher than was possible even a few decades ago.

Although it was an outlier in terms of its popularity, the success of Instagram is illustrative of the productivity that modern software engineering teams can achieve. Development of Instagram began in early 2010, with the first photo posted on July 16, 2010. By the time of its acquisition by Facebook for $1 billion in April, 2012, the service had about 30 million users but only 13 employees [2]. The rapid development and growth that Instagram's team accomplished was due in large part to the availability of high-level programming languages that offer powerful abstractions, as well as open source libraries that obviated the need to build tools from scratch.[1]

While you probably do not aspire to build the next popular photo-sharing service, this example shows the power that becomes available to you when you become familiar with software development tools and best practices.

2.1.2 Collaboration Across Time and Space

Even if you are working alone on a research project, if you are using open source software then you are in some sense collaborating with other developers. "Open source" in this context means software for which the original source code is freely available to read, use, and in some cases modify and redistribute. It includes many popular programming languages such as Python and R, as well as many libraries built on top of them. Leveraging open source tools means that if you encounter a common problem, such as fitting a linear model or building a simple website, there are probably many pre-existing solutions that you can adapt to your needs.

You can think of this type of collaboration as collaborating across time, building on previous achievements. The second type of collaboration, which is in some ways easier to picture, occurs when you are working with a team of other programmers toward a common goal. This type of collaboration involves several (in some cases, very many) developers each writing code on different computers but wanting to keep their changes in sync.

You may have experienced this in other contexts such as preparing a group presentation. One popular approach for addressing this is to introduce a naming scheme to your files, such as `version1.ppt`, `version2.ppt`, and so on. If you have spent much time on such efforts, you have likely encountered examples such as `presentation_final_FINAL.ppt` and `presentation_final_FINAL-NO-REALLY.ppt`. This highlights the difficulty of tracking changes and keeping an authoritative version of a document with distributed authorship. Because this is such a common problem for teams writing software, several popular solutions have been developed. The next section describes these tools and explains how to use one that we recommend.

2.2 Source Control

The text files that software developers write are called "source code." The process of writing this code often takes months or years and can be distributed over a team of hundreds, as described in the previous section. To help manage these challenges,

---

[1] Readers may be interested to note that the server side application backing Instagram's popular mobile applications was written in Python.

many types of source control have been developed. The most popular version control tools today include Concurrent Version Systems (CVS), Subversion (SVN), and Git.

Version control has several advantages:

- tracking changes in files over time
- allowing multiple authors to edit the same file and reconcile their changes
- maintaining a set of files together as a project

Tracking changes is the minimal requirement for a version control system. Being able to view the history of a project and its contents will allow you to see what changed, when, and who changed it. Over the course of a long-running project, being able to review these changes and any associated documentation will give you more context for why certain actions were taken.

If you are collaborating with other developers, there will often be cases where more than one person edits the same file within a period of time. Reconciling these changes becomes easier when you have tracked what changed and when. There can still be difficulties when two (or more) authors edit the same exact line in different ways in quick succession, but version control will surface these conflicts and allow you to resolve them.

Version control also helps to share a project's *structure* in addition to its contents. If you send a zip file of documents to another person, they can re-organize them on their computer in a way that prevents them from working as intended. With version control, the project itself becomes a logical unit that can be shared, preserving its organization even when copies exist in many different locations.

The version control system that we recommend and describe here is Git. It has become very popular in recent years in large part due to the existence of GitHub, which offers free and paid hosting options for projects that use Git as their version control system.[2] GitHub and similar sites such as GitLab have made Git popular for many uses besides software development. GitHub projects now include examples such as musical composition,[3] recipes,[4] and legal documents.[5] One of the most interesting examples is the use of GitHub by the German Bundestag to maintain an unofficial copy of its legislation with easy tracking of historical changes.[6]

2.2.1 Getting Started with Git

Git was designed by Linus Torvalds, who also lent his name to the Linux operating system [1]. Because Linux is a very large open source software project, Linus and the many other developers needed a way to manage changes to the software that

---

[2]https://github.com/.
[3]https://github.com/CMAA/nova-organi-harmonia.
[4]https://github.com/hadley/recipes.
[5]https://github.com/twitter/innovators-patent-agreement.
[6]https://github.com/bundestag/gesetze.

could be easily incorporated into a final version for distribution. To achieve this, Git uses a concept of "branching," which we will discuss in a moment.

We will use Git as our source control tool throughout this book. In fact, the authors used Git and GitHub to collaborate on the authorship of the book itself.

2.2.1.1 Creating Your First GitHub Repository

Although a GitHub account is not essential for working with Git, it provides an easy and natural way to get started. To sign up for a free GitHub account, visit https://github.com/join. At the time of writing, GitHub also offers free private hosting for students as part of their Student Developer Pack (see https://education.github.com/pack).

After creating your account, you are ready to set up your first repository (or "repo"). A repository is analogous to a project, and consists of a directory with metadata stored in a `.git` subdirectory. You can initialize Git tracking in an existing folder on your computer by entering the command `git init` in your terminal. However, GitHub also provides a way to initialize repositories online and then clone them to your computer. That method is a bit easier for beginners, so that is what we describe here.

On your GitHub home page (`github.com/your_username`), choose "New repository" under the create ("+") menu. Give the repository a name that will be easy for you to remember and type at the command line, such as `myfirstrepo`. You can also give it a short description, such as "Getting started." For now, do not select the option to initialize the repository with a README file or license.

After creating the repository, you will be taken to a page with instructions on how to clone it to your computer. Cloning is the process of copying a remote repository (one that exists on another computer, in this case GitHub's servers) to your local machine. We recommend that you follow the instructions to clone the repository via the command line. Tools like GitHub Desktop or Git Tower are applications that allow you to manage your repositories via a graphical interface, but we suggest that you become comfortable with basic Git commands in your terminal first. This will give you a better understanding of what is happening and allow you to work with Git in environments where graphical applications are unavailable (such as on remote servers) if needed.

Once you have cloned the repository and located it in your terminal, you can list its contents (`$ ls -a`) and see that it is empty other than the `.git` subdirectory that we mentioned above. If you chose to initialize a local repository without using GitHub, this is equivalent to creating a new directory and running the `$ git init` command inside it. The next section describes how to begin tracking your changes in the repository.

2.2 Source Control

2.2.1.2 Committing Changes

Now that you have a (virtually) empty repository, it is time to add a file and make some changes. At any given time, files can be in one of four states with respect to Git:

- untracked
- unstaged changes
- staged changes
- unmodified

Untracked files are ones that Git is not watching for version control purposes. This is analogous to opening a new document in a word processor but not saving it—the contents exist, but they are not being tracked in a file.

Files with unstaged changes are ones that Git is tracking but that have not been added to the staging area. Git's staging area allows you to prepare and review a set of changes before committing them. Staged changes are ones that have been added to a changeset but not yet committed.

Committing changes is the process of creating a commit in your Git history. A commit is a logical set of changes accompanied by a unique identifier, a timestamp of when the commit occurred, a record of who created the commit (name and email address), and the changes that were applied to the repository.

Generally speaking, your changes will proceed in the order described above: from untracked, to unstaged, to staged, to committed. You can always check the status of files in a Git repo with the `$ git status` command. This will show which files are untracked, which have unstaged changes, and which are staged for the next commit. Unmodified files (ones whose current state is committed in the repository) are not shown by default.

To start tracking a new file in your repository, create a simple file such as a text file. If your repository is at the path ~/myrepository (equivalent to /Users/{your username}/myrepository/ on a Unix-based system such as MacOS), you can create a text file in that directory by navigating to that path (`cd ~/myrepository`) and using the `touch` command to make an empty file (`touch myfile.txt`). Re-run `$ git status` to verify that the file exists but is untracked. (Notice that the status message below the filename says something like "nothing added to commit but untracked files present.")

Then, add it to the staging area for a commit:

```
$ git add myfile.txt
```

Run `$ git status` again to see the file listed under "changes to be committed."

To create your commit using these changes, you want to run some variant of the `git commit` command. This opens a text editor in which to record your commit message. By default this uses the `vi` editor, which may be unfamiliar to many readers.[7] Many first-time Git users are confused by `vi` and it can get in the way of creating useful commit messages. Instead, we suggest using the `-m` option to supply your commit message at the command line:

```
git commit -m "my first commit"
```

Once we commit, this flushes the change set and creates "first commit" in the Git log. A commit represents a set of changes to files—it is *not* the files themselves. This is good because it allows you to merge multiple commits (sets of changes) to the same file, often with little or no conflict. Because a commit represents changes, it can also be undone or "reverted."

Now your Git status will show no unmodified files ("nothing to commit, working directory clean").

To see the details associated with your commit message, use the `git log` command. You will see something similar to the following:

```
commit 1da177e4c3f41524e886b7f1b8a0c1fc7321cac2
Author: Your Name <name@mail.com>
Date:   Sat Apr 16 09:54:06 2005 -0700

    my first commit
```

The first line shows the unique identifier (usually referred to as a SHA, for the secure hashing algorithm that produces it) of the commit. The second line contains the author details, which in this case reflects your local Git configuration. The third line contains the timestamp of when the change occurred, including the author's timezone as an offset from UTC time. The next line is the commit message.

Writing good commit messages is a matter of style, and speaks to the collaborative aspect of software development that we discussed above. Although there is no theoretical limit to the length of a commit message, most messages range from one line to a few short paragraphs. We recommend the following as best practices for commit messages:

- Provide a one sentence summary at the beginning describing the main idea of the change
- List more granular changes below the summary, one per line
- Your specific changes should use the imperative present tense to describe what the commit does ("Add support for..." rather than "Added...," "Adds...," or "I added...")
- Keep the commit to one main idea (if you find yourself using the word "and" a lot, it is probably best to break it into separate commits)

Of course, this is a stylistic decision and the preferred style may differ depending on your collaborators. If you are working with a group of other programmers,

---

[7] You can configure which editor uses by setting the `GIT_EDITOR` or `EDITOR` environment variables on your system. Advanced Git configuration is outside the scope of this book, but you can find more info in Sec. 10.8 of [1].

discuss this up front so that your messages will be in a similar style to ensure a readable Git history for your project.

2.2.1.3 Distributed Version Control: Pushing and Pulling

Another key idea behind Git is that it is "distributed version control." This means that there is no one canonical version of a repository living on a server somewhere—any copy of the code on someone's machine is equally valid in the eyes of git. Because of this, you can "push" and "pull" code to and from multiple other places.

To get started with an existing repository, you use the command `git clone` followed by the location of the repository such as

```
git clone
    https://github.com/{username}/{repository_name}.git
```

or

```
git clone
    git@github.com:{username}/{repository_name}.git
```

The first method above uses HTTP and the second uses SSH. If you create your repository directly through the GitHub web interface, you can get the exact URI that you need to pass to the `git clone` command from the "Clone or download" dropdown on the main page for the repository.[8]

Now that you have committed changes, you can push them to GitHub with the following command:

```
git push origin master
```

This command pushes (uploads) the changes to the remote location known as "origin" (in this case, your repository on GitHub's servers) using the "master" branch. We will discuss more about branches in the next section.

To get changes from others into our local version, we pull:

```
git pull origin
```

The key idea here is that you can push to and pull from arbitrary places. It is easy to think of what is on GitHub as the "true" version of your repository, but that is no more authoritative a source than your local repository. GitHub is simply a service that makes it convenient to store your code in a place that is accessible, along with a nice interface for viewing the details of your project. Once you have pushed your changes, visit your repository's page on GitHub to view the same info that we saw using the `git log` command above.

---

[8]On recent versions of MacOS, you may need to run `xcode-select --install` in your terminal (not the Python console) before running any Git commands.

2.2.1.4 A Word on Branching

Another powerful concept in Git is the idea of branches. Branching allows you to maintain multiple threads of work. This is useful because you often want to work on two things in concert, such as expanding an existing codebase while keeping an earlier version stable. If you are tracking the work for a presentation in a Git repo, for example, you might want to create different branches as you change the formatting for different occasions. If you want to combine the branches later you do this by merging them, which allows you to share changes across branches.[9]

To start a new branch and begin work on it, we have to check it out:

```
git branch mynewbranch
git checkout mynewbranch
```

The first command creates the branch in your Git metadata, and the second command sets that as the branch you are working on. There is also a shortcut to perform both of these steps simultaneously: `git checkout -b mynewbranch`. You can "checkout" any branch that you have created (or fetched) locally. Checking out the master branch works the same as any other branch: you can run `git checkout master`.

You can see the list of local Git branches in your repository by running the `git branch` command. The currently checked out branch will be indicated with an asterisk. You can have many branches on your system, but you can only have one checked out at a time. To verify this, open the same Git repository in two terminal windows. Checkout a new branch in one of the windows, and then run the `git branch` command in the other—you will see that it is using the same branch that you just checked out.

In the example above, we pushed to the master branch of your new repository. You can also push non-master branches:

```
git push origin mynewbranch
```

In the same way that there is no one authoritative copy of a Git repository, "master" is just a convenient naming convention. This branch is not special in any way other than by convention, and we could just as easily call the main branch "main" or "primary." Almost every Git project uses "master" though, so that is what most people are used to.

When we are ready to merge two branches, check out the "destination" branch (usually master). Then run the `git merge` command to merge the other branch into this one.

```
git checkout master
git merge mynewbranch
```

---

[9]There are other ways to share changes between branches without merging them, such as cherry-picking, that we do not cover here.

Git uses a merge algorithm to apply the changes from mynewbranch into master in this case. In some instances, both branches will have changes to the same line of a file. In these cases you will see merge conflicts. You must resolve these one-by-one by choosing which changes to keep before completing the merge.

Why might you use branches instead of making all your changes on the master branch? Suppose that you are the maintainer of an R package on CRAN. If the currently released version of your package is 1.0, you may decide to create a new branch to begin working on the next version, 1.1 or 2.0. In the meantime, if someone discovers a bug in 1.0 that you need to fix, you will have to switch back to this version to make your changes. Without branching this could be a major headache but with branching it becomes a much easier process.

2.2.1.5 Practical Tips for Using Git

Before we close this section we want to offer two more practical suggestions for using git.

The first is to keep your commits fairly fine-grained. One commit should be a single idea, a bug fix, or a small feature. It should be complete so that you can undo or redo the commit with minimal worrying. A basic rule of thumb is: if you cannot describe what you did in a single line, it is too big a jump.

Our second recommendation for Git is to do some exploration online so you can take advantage of all it has to offer. There is a lot of great documentation, and Github is free. One feature to get you started is the .gitignore file. Search online for this and think about (or discuss in class) how you might use it. If you would like to learn more about how Git works, check out [1], which was also written using Git and Github.

2.3 Lab Session

Most lab sessions will start in the same way: with a short script of starter code and a set of instructions. The instructions will specify parts of the starter code that are broken and need to be fixed, and/or functions and commands that should be added to the code in order to make it run properly. Later in the book the lab instructions will be at a more conceptual level, and require participants to work out the implementation details themselves.

Each lab is meant to fill about 1–1.5 h. However, do not worry if there is not enough time to complete all of the material. Often the basic idea of the lab can be grasped in the first few exercises, and the later ones build on this. If desired, unfinished portions of the lab can be assigned in addition to the homework. After a lecture on the concepts discussed in the chapter and completion of the lab exercises, students should be prepared to complete the homework.

If the material in the preceding chapter is not sufficient to solve the challenges in lab, participants are encouraged to find online resources to bridge the gap. This process of finding documentation online is a prominent part of most programmers' workflow, and students should not be embarrassed about doing so. Note that this is quite different from trying to find exact solutions that can be copied and pasted.

We recommend working through the first homework assignment during the lab session this week. The learning curve can be steep for readers unfamiliar with Git. Review the concepts introduced in this chapter, and have students help one another set up their GitHub accounts and local repositories.

Homework

This homework is meant to get you comfortable using Git on your own machine.

Create a Github Account

Following the steps described in the chapter above, create a free account on GitHub if you do not already have one. During this process, you will need to set up SSH keys on the machine that you plan to access GitHub from. While GitHub has great documentation for getting started, setting up SSH is a somewhat arcane step.[10] *Do not get stuck here.* If you find yourself getting hung up ask one of your classmates or your instructor for help.

Fork an Existing Project

"Forking" a project on GitHub allows you to copy over the project and all of its associated changesets. By forking a project you will then have your own copy and any changes that you submit will not be committed to the original repository.
Find an existing project on GitHub that you are interested in forking. This could be an R or Python library, such as https://github.com/tidyverse/ggplot2 or https://github.com/scikit-learn/scikit-learn. It could also be a project directly related to social science such as https://github.com/openeventdata/political-actor-recommendation or https://github.com/bundestag/gesetze. Create a fork in the GitHub user interface in order to create a copy on your GitHub account.

Clone the Forked Project

After you have forked your chosen project go to GitHub page for your forked copy. Using the designated URL, clone the repository to your local machine. Use the

---
[10]https://help.github.com/en/articles/adding-a-new-ssh-key-to-your-github-account.

same command that we illustrated above when copying the first repository that you created.

Review the History

Using the `git log` command, review the history of the project and answer the following questions:

1. When was the most recent commit created?
2. What is the unique identifier (SHA) of the most recent commit?
3. Who created the most recent commit?
4. When was the earliest commit created? (For very old projects, go back some arbitrary number of commits such as 100.)
5. Who created the earliest commit?
6. Approximately how many commits and contributors does the project have? (For small projects you can see this in the Git log, for very large projects it will be easier to find this in the GitHub UI.)

Navigating GitHub

If possible, find the GitHub accounts of the authors of the first and last commits of the repo you forked.

7. How many public repositories do they each have?
8. What is their most starred repository? (Stars are a way for GitHub users to indicate interest in or endorsement of a repository; they are not a feature of Git itself.)

Push a Change

Make a small change to one file in the forked project and push it to your remote repository (on GitHub).

9. Provide a link to the commit in your forked repository. It should have your username, the repository name, and the commit identifier (SHA) in the URL.

References

1. Chacon, S., & Straub, B. (2014). *Pro git*. New York: Apress.
2. Swisher, K. (2013). *The money shot*. Retrieved March 24, 2018, from https://www.vanityfair.com/news/business/2013/06/kara-swisher-instagram

Chapter 3
Object-Oriented Programming

There are three major paradigms for designing software: procedural, functional, and object-oriented design. All three approaches use common features such as variables, data structures, and functions. The key difference is in which levels of abstraction are emphasized in each paradigm.

In procedural (or imperative) programming, the focus is on functions, routines, and subroutines (collectively known as procedures). Languages in this category include C, FORTRAN, Pascal, and R. The major advantage of procedural languages over their antecedents was the ability to group logically related behavior into a unit of abstraction (a function, something like `square_root(4)`) rather than by its entry point in the code (`GOTO 100`, meaning run the code block starting on line 100). Procedural programming is sufficient for small projects. However, it becomes difficult to use for larger projects because there is very little hierarchy or structure.

Another paradigm is functional programming, which treats all computation as the evaluation of mathematical functions. The most well-known example of a functional programming language is Lisp. Some nice aspects of functional programming (list comprehensions and lambda expressions) have been incorporated into Python. A more strict type of functional programming, known as "purely functional" programming, uses functions with no side effects (they do not affect the state of the program in any way other than producing output) and immutable data structures. As a beginner it is enough to know that functional programming exists, and other than that you do not need to concern yourself with it for now.

The third way is to view the world as a set of objects, hence the moniker object-oriented programming (OOP). OOP tightly couples data with methods that can be performed on it. This is the approach we will take in this book. In addition to

---

Electronic Supplementary Material The online version of this chapter (https://doi.org/10.1007/978-3-030-36826-5_3) contains supplementary material, which is available to authorized users.

© Springer Nature Switzerland AG 2020
J. Cutler, M. Dickenson, *Computational Frameworks for Political and Social Research with Python*, Textbooks on Political Analysis,
https://doi.org/10.1007/978-3-030-36826-5_3

Python, other object-oriented programming languages include Java and Ruby. The remainder of this chapter discusses details of the object-oriented paradigm and how it helps us think about developing software.

3.1 Object-Oriented Design

The big idea of OOP in Python is that *everything is an object*. This includes variables and classes. Object-oriented design uses *classes* as models of the world, and particular digital examples of these classes are known as *instances*. Understanding how these three concepts—objects, methods, and classes—relate to one another is the key to object-oriented programming, but it can be difficult to grok at first.[1] Working through examples will help you to understand how this abstraction is a powerful way to design and organize software.

3.1.1 Objects, Classes, and Instances

Objects are the easiest part to understand by analogy to the physical world. Every object in the physical world has two characteristics: *state* and *behavior*. For example, your current state includes your name, age, and emotions (perhaps bored or confused at the moment). Your behavior includes all the actions you can undertake (not just the ones you are currently engaged in): eating, sleeping, reading, programming, and so on.

A class is the blueprint for creating objects. Continuing with our example of people, we could have Human as a class. Starting from this basic template, we could set up our Human class so that all objects based on this class will have certain state and behavior properties. In creating a class we set up the presence of state variables, not their values. In other words, we specify that all Humans will have a name and an age, but we do not set the value of those names and ages at the class level (although we could specify defaults). We also include common behaviors at the class level. Creating classes forces you to think about the essence of the concept you are trying to represent.[2]

One thing to be careful about in this example is the formatting of the __init__ function. Make sure that the word init has two underscores before it and two

---

[1] Grok, coined in [1] means roughly "to understand intuitively."

[2] Note that unlike the previous chapter, many of the code snippets in this chapter begin with line numbers rather than >>>. This is meant to indicate that we expect the code to be saved in Python files, which are plain-text files with a .py extension such as my_code.py. We recommend typing the code into an editor of your choice and running it with a command such as python my_code.py. This will allow you to save your code for later, and to easily edit it if you make any mistakes.

3.1 Object-Oriented Design

more after it. This is the convention for functions that in Python are known as "magic methods." The difference between these and other methods that you might define in Python is that "magic methods" are not called directly. In other words, you would likely never call `Human.__init__()`. Instead, this method gets called implicitly when you initialize an instance of the class with `Human()`. We discuss magic methods further in Sect. 3.1.2. For now, just be careful to put underscores in the function name of your initializer.

```
1  class Human(object):
2      def __init__(self, name=""):  # notice the default
            for name
3          self.name = name
4
5      def intro(self):
6          print("Hi, I'm " + self.name)
```

Finally, we also have instances: unique instantiations of a class that represent an object. You and I are each unique instantiations of the class Human. We share certain traits, but also have many features that we do not share. As a programmer, you often form expectations about the behavior of an instance based on its class. Continuing our example above (the line numbering continues, indicating that you are intended to write this in the same file as the code immediately above), notice how we use the Human class to create two separate instances with similar features but different values:

```
8  josh = Human("Josh")
9  josh.intro()
10 matt = Human("Matt")
11 matt.name                  # 'Matt'
12 matt.name == josh.name     # False
13 type(matt) == type(josh)   # True
```

3.1.2 Example: Fibonacci Numbers

To get a clearer picture of how the object-oriented paradigm works, we will go through another example. Fibonacci numbers are integers in the sequence $0, 1, 1, 2, 3, 5, 8\ldots$ defined such that $F_0 = 0, F_1 = 1$, and $F_n = F_{n-1} + F_{n-2}$. Because all Fibonacci numbers share this same formula, we can set up this behavior in a class:

fib.py:

```
1  class Fib(object):
2      def __init__(self):
3          self.last = 0
```

```
 4              self.second = 0
 5
 6      def next_fib(self):
 7          if self.last == 0:
 8              self.last = 1
 9              return 0
10
11          current = self.last
12          self.last = self.second + self.last
13          self.second = current
14          return current
```

Again, we encourage you to type this code into a plain-text file with a name like `fib.py`. You can copy and paste it into the Python console or run it from your shell with `$ python fib.py`.

Once you know more about how a class is set up in Python, you can verify for yourself that this code meets the definition of a Fibonacci number. First, we specify that we are setting up a **class** (line 1) the same way that we use **def** to indicate that we are about to define a function. In this case, the class is named `Fib`. The reference to **object** in parentheses denotes that our new class *inherits* from the **object** class. We will discuss inheritance more below.

Next (on line 2) we create a *constructor* with `__init__`.[3] This method is called whenever a new instance of the class is created. You *must* pass the `self` variable, and you can specify additional arguments (as we did with `name` in the `Human` example above). The `self` variable is used to refer to the object itself internally.[4] This can be useful since we do not know the name of any instances at the time we are defining the class. In this initializer, we give all instances of the class two local variables, `last` and `second`.

Lines 6 and below define the function `next_fib()`. Note that we have to pass `self` to this function, so that it can access `self.last` and `self.second`. Because this function belongs to the class `Fib`, we call it a Fib "method." All of the data types that you have used so far in Python—lists, strings, numbers, and so on—are all objects. Examples of methods you have used so far might include calling **len**() on a list or string and **abs**(), **int**(), or **float**() on a number.

---

[3] Remember that methods beginning and ending with the double-underscore are called "magic methods" and are built into Python. The opposite of an initializer is called a destructor and can be designated with `__del__`. A very useful magic method is `__str__`, which defines what will be returned when an object is printed. We will see an example of this in the lab session later in the chapter.

[4] In fact you can use any variable name to refer to the instance as long as it is the first argument to the function, but by convention Python programmers use `self` and so tools such as text editors understand this convention for the purpose of syntax highlighting.

3.1 Object-Oriented Design

We set up the class with two default values, `self.last` and `self.second`. These are the state variables for our `Fib` class. `Fib` also has one behavior, `next_fib()`, which generates the next number in the sequence.

To be able to use the code we have defined in our file within an interactive Python session, we must import it. This is very similar to how we would include third-party code. From within the same directory as your `fib.py` file, start a new Python session. Then, run the import command (**import** `fib`) and use your `Fib` class as below:

```
>>> import fib
>>> fib1 = fib.Fib()
>>> fib1.next_fib()      # 0
>>> fib1.next_fib()      # 1
>>> fib2 = fib.Fib()
>>> fib2.next_fib()      # 0
>>> fib2.next_fib()      # 1
>>> fib2.next_fib()      # 1
>>> fib2.next_fib()      # 2
>>> fib2.next_fib()      # 3
```

If you see an `ImportError` with a message like `No module named 'fib'`, make sure that you are launching the Python interpreter from the folder that contains your `fib.py` file. For example, if your `fib.py` file is in a folder at `/Users/user1/code/`, make sure to navigate to that directory in your terminal (`cd /Users/user1/code/`) before starting Python with the `python` command.

Here we have a complete (albeit simple) example of object-oriented design. Objects `fib1` and `fib2` are instances of the class `Fib()`, which defined the variables they would have (state) and a method that could be called (behavior).

Note that Python caches imports, so if you change the code in `fib.py` and re-run **import** `fib`, nothing will happen. To force the code to reload, you can run **from** `importlib` **import** `reload` and then **reload**(foo).

3.1.3 Inheritance and Polymorphism

In the example above, we said that our `Fib` class inherited from **object**, but what did that mean? To help understand this better, we will use another example to demonstrate inheritance. Python is a method-passing language, which means it does something called "dynamic dispatch." Say we define a generic class Animal and a more specific class Cat that inherits from Animal:

polymorphism.py:

```
1  class Animal(object):
2      def __init__(self, name):       # Constructor of the class
```

```
3              self.name = name
4
5      def talk(self):                    # Abstract method,
       defined by convention only
6          raise NotImplementedError("Subclass must
       implement abstract method")
7
8  class Cat(Animal):
9      def talk(self):
10         return self.meow()
11
12     def meow(self):
13         return 'Meow!'
14
15 class Dog(Animal):
16     def talk(self):
17         return self.bark()
18
19     def bark(self):
20         return 'Woof! Woof!'
21
22 class Fish(Animal):
23
24     def swim(self):
25         pass
26
27     def __str__(self):
28         return "I am a fish!"
29
30     def talk(self):
31         return '...'
32
33 animals = [Cat('Foo'),
34            Dog('Bar'),
35            Fish('nemo')]
36
37 for animal in animals:
38     print(animal.name + ': ' + animal.talk())
39
40
41 f = Fish("foo")
42 print("Hi, " + str(f))
```

We have created a class Animal with the basic trait (state variable) name. In other words, our abstraction of animals dictates that all Animals have names. We

3.1 Object-Oriented Design

then create a second class Cat, which has all the state variables and behaviors of Animals, as well as some more specific properties. Notice that we did not have to define our __init__ function again in the Cat class—it will perform exactly the same as in the Animal class.

In this case, Animal is the "superclass" of Cat, and Cat is a "subclass" of Animal. What is the superclass of Animal? That's right, It is **object**, and Animal is a subclass of **object**.

So if we do the following, what happens? If you are not sure, try it for yourself before reading the answer. Instead of running **import** polymorphism as we did with the fib example above, run **from** polymorphism **import** *. This will allow you to use the classes such as Animal directly, without having to refer to them as polymorphism.Animal. Alternatively, you could specify each class in the import statement such as **from** polymorphism **import** Animal, Cat, but **from** polymorphism **import** * can be a useful shortcut.

```
>>> a = Animal("Fido")
>>> b = Cat("Sally")
>>> b.talk()
```

When we call the method b.talk(), it will search within class Cat first, and then class Animal if it does not find anything. This is known as *polymorphism*, but it will not mean much to you until you practice. There is a trade-off between generality and specificity in how much you want a subclass to inherit from a superior class. Practicing this will force you to think about:

- What should exist at the object level?
- How should those things interact with each other?

3.1.4 Design Choices

Object-oriented programming evolved as a paradigm in response to common problems faced by developers in earlier programming languages. Since virtually everything about a program is within our control as developers, design choices are omnipresent in programming. As the paradox of choice suggests, sometimes this flexibility is overwhelming and counterproductive, so conventions and heuristics have emerged to help make these choices easier [2].

Examples of design choices you will face include:

- how to give variables informative names (e.g., mean_gdp instead of x)
- what to call your functions and which parameters they should take (e.g., do you take the number of observations in your data set as an argument, or do you compute it within your function)
- how to organize the files in your project (e.g., whether to put code and data into the same folder or separate subfolders)

When you face these design decisions it can be helpful to fall back on first principles. One question you can ask yourself to aid in your decision is, "does doing this convey knowledge about my understanding of the world?" For example, calling a variable x in your program forces anyone reading your code to figure out what it does. If you know at the time you write the code that it represents a useful quantity such as per-capita GDP, give your reader an indication of that in how you name the variable.

A second useful question to ask yourself is, "would this decision surprise another developer?" This one will be harder to answer as a beginner, but you will understand it through practice and by reading other people's code. One simple way to answer this as a beginner is to ask a collaborator—a classmate, an instructor, or someone else who can understand the context of your project—what they think about your decision.

The third heuristic you can use is, "will I remember in 6 months why I made this decision?" The first time that you touch a piece of code is when you will have the most context in your head for what it should do. Make it easy for your future self by writing clear code and adding comments to help explain the intended behavior. This is a skill that you will get better at over time, but it is good to begin practicing now.

3.2 Why OOP?

There are a number of compelling reasons to use object-oriented design in your programming. Many of these will already be apparent to you after reviewing the examples above, but some do not become obvious until you work on larger projects. Since OOP is the way we will write code in this book, we owe you an explanation of some of these benefits.

All of the classes we created in the last section shared a common purpose. Did you notice what it was? One of our goals was to avoid repetition when creating objects. This is known as the **DRY** principle: Do not Repeat Yourself. By employing this principle (and OOP more generally), you will be writing more efficient code—doing more with less—even though it may not feel that way at first.

A second advantage of OOP is that it allows you to define *interfaces*. This means that we can use certain methods without worrying about how they work—we just know that we can call them and what the expected behavior is. Another great thing about interfaces is that we can change the implementation "under the hood," and as long as our tests still pass our users will not have to worry. Interfaces will be useful later when we discuss querying data sources such as Facebook and Twitter—we do not have to know how the service works, just which method calls to make to obtain what we need.

Polymorphism (known formally as "subtype polymorphism") is what makes interfaces possible. All subclasses can be responsible for their own implementation of certain behaviors. For example, if you continued with the Dog subclass as suggested, you probably defined a bark() method. We could have created a more general `talk()` method at the Animal level, but not doing so allowed us some flexibility. Variables and methods should be named in a sensible way, meaning that they are easy to remember and clearly readable in code. By convention, class names are capitalized (`Animal`), variable names are lower-cased (`fido`), and function names are "snake-cased" (`compute_square_root()`).

Another reason to like interfaces, and OOP in general, is because they allow for *encapsulation* of code. In each of the examples above, all of our state variables (variables referred to by `self.`) belong to the instances and have to be accessed that way. That means if we create `fido = Animal("Fido")` and then inspect the variable `name`, it will not be set—there is no global variable called `name`. Only when we access `fido.name` can we get the name of our Animal. If we wanted to hide any of our variables (by making them "private") we could preface them with two underscores, such as `self.__age`. Variables named in this way cannot be accessed directly, unlike `fido.name`. Encapsulation also means that all of our data and their methods stay together; we never have to worry about where to find the `meow` function for a cat—it can always be called right from the instances themselves.

Most of these OOP advantages come down to being able to say, "This is a `thing`. It should have `this` info and `these` methods." Any code can be written procedurally *or* as OOP, but we should choose whichever is simpler. For the projects in this book, OOP is preferable for the reasons listed above. The lab section and homework this week will help you get more comfortable with object-oriented design and Python conventions for writing object-oriented code.

3.3 Lab Session

3.3.1 Review: Python Functions and Magic Methods

At the beginning of lab, discuss each of the following functions and make sure everyone understands how they work and what they do:

1. **import** and **from...import** (loading libraries)
2. **class** (defining a class)
3. **object** (the most fundamental class in Python)
4. **__init__** (behavior that happens when an instance of a class is initialized)
5. **__str__** and **__repr__** (what happens when an instance is printed or otherwise asked to represent itself as a string)
6. **self** (keyword for referring to an instance in method definitions)
7. **dict()**, and the key/value pattern (casting a value to a dictionary)
8. **split** (turning a string into a list of substrings)
9. **range** (getting a list of integers with specified endpoints)
10. **zip** (combining multiple lists)
11. **min** and **max** (minimum and maximum value in a list)

12. **sum** (total value of a list)
13. **len** (size of a list)
14. **lambda** (a one-line expression)
15. **while** (iterate until a stopping condition is met)

3.3.2 Example: The Median Voter Theorem

For background on this week's lab, refresh your understanding of the Median Voter Theorem.[5] You might also be interested in the trivia associated with the proposed U.S. state of Jefferson.[6]

In this lab session, we will demonstrate (through simulation) an example of the median voter theorem. In the following code, we have classes for making an Individual and a Candidate. Which is the superclass, and which is the subclass?

   mvt.py:

```
1  """
2  Lab 2: Classes and Inheritance
3  Demonstrating the Median Voter Theorem
4  """
5  import random
6  from matplotlib import pyplot
7  import numpy as np
8  from scipy.stats import gaussian_kde
9
10
11 class Individual(object):
12     def __init__(self, ideology):
13         self.ideology = ideology
14
15 class Voter(Individual):
16     def __init__(self, ideology):
17         Individual.__init__(self, ideology)
18
19
20 class Candidate(Individual):
21     def __init__(self, ideology, party):
22         Individual.__init__(self, ideology)
23         self.old_ideology = self.ideology
```

---

[5] http://en.wikipedia.org/wiki/Median_voter_theorem.
[6] http://en.wikipedia.org/wiki/Jefferson_(Pacific_state).

```
24              self.party = party
25              self.numerator = 1
26              self.denominator = 1
27
28          def __repr__(self):
29              return "%s party" % self.party
30
31          def report_ideology(self):
32              return self.ideology
33
34          def update_ideology(self, ballot):
35              pass
36
37
38  class Polity(object):
39      def __init__(self):
40          self.voters = []
41          self.candidates = []
42
43      def populate(self, count):
44          for _ in range(count):
45              ideol = random.betavariate(5, 5)
46              voter = Voter(ideol)
47              self.voters.append(voter)
48
49      def nominate(self, cand):
50          self.candidates.append(cand)
51
52      def election(self):
53          counts = [0] * len(self.candidates)
54          ballots = dict(zip(self.candidates, counts))
55          for voter in self.voters:
56              min_diff = min(range(len(self.candidates)),
57                             key=lambda i:
        abs(voter.ideology - self.candidates[i].ideology))
58              choice = self.candidates[min_diff]
59              ballots[choice] += 1
60          return ballots
61
62      def get_winner(self, ballots):
63          winner = max(ballots, key=ballots.get)
64          return winner
65
66      def report_candidate_ideologies(self):
```

```
67          for candidate in self.candidates:
68              print(candidate, ":",
        candidate.report_ideology())
69
70      def update_candidate_ideologies(self, ballot):
71          pass
72
73      def plot_voter_ideologies(self):
74          ids = []
75          for voter in self.voters:
76              ids.append(voter.ideology)
77          density = gaussian_kde(ids)
78          x_vals = np.linspace(0, 1, 200)
79          density.covariance_factore = lambda: .25
80          density._compute_covariance()
81          pyplot.plot(x_vals, density(x_vals))
82          pyplot.savefig('voter-ideologies.png')
83          pyplot.close()
84
85      def plot_candidate_ideologies(self, vertical=1):
86          x_vals = [candidate.report_ideology() for
        candidate in self.candidates]
87          y_vals = [vertical] * len(x_vals)
88          pyplot.axis([0.0, 1.0, 0.5, vertical+0.5])
89          axis = pyplot.gca()
90          axis.set_autoscale_on(False)
91          pyplot.plot([0, 1], [vertical, vertical], '-')
92          colors = 'b,g,r,c,m,y,k,w'.split(',')
93          colors = colors[0:len(x_vals)]
94          pyplot.scatter(x_vals, y_vals, marker='o',
        color=colors, s=150)
95
96  def print_winner(winner):
97      print("And the winner is... the %s!" % winner)
98
99  def run_election(polity):
100     result = polity.election()
101     print(result)
102     winner = polity.get_winner(result)
103     print_winner(winner)
104     print("OLD IDEOLOGIES:")
105     polity.report_candidate_ideologies()
106     polity.plot_candidate_ideologies()
107     print("NEW IDEOLOGIES:")
```

```
108      polity.update_candidate_ideologies(result)
109      polity.report_candidate_ideologies()
110      print("\n")
111      return winner
```

Based on this example, complete the Voter class by having a voter tell you their ideology when printed (hint: remember the magic methods).

Next we introduce another class: Polity. It has three key methods: populate, nominate, and election. Read through each and discuss how they work. How do these behaviors modify the state of the Polity? What values do they return? Are there any potentially undesirable side effects that should be handled?

Do not worry for now about the plotting functions. There is one function to plot the voters' ideologies along a one-dimensional scale, and another to plot the candidates' positions on the same scale. It is not essential that you understand how this works right now. We will discuss plotting in more detail in the next chapter.

Now it is time for election night. Initialize candidates from each of the five parties. Create a Polity with 100 voters, and nominate the candidates. Who do you think will win the election? Why?

Simulate the election and see whether the guesses were correct.

Now, form groups of 2–3 lab participants each and complete the following tasks:

3.1

(a) Implement missing print methods in Voter and Polity.
(b) Initialize candidates from other parties.
(c) Nominate the new candidates.
(d) Implement update_ideology() in the Candidate class by which they adjust their ideology to appeal to the voters. The key constraint is that Candidates cannot access voters' ideology—they can only "learn" from the ballot in the election. (Notice that you might have to adjust this method slightly.) Note that we treat ideology as a numerical rather than a categorical variable in this example.
(e) Implement update_candidate_ideologies() in the Polity class.
(f) Implement a loop to run elections until the Sensible Party loses.

To conclude the lab session, review the images produced by the simulations. What can we learn from this result? How might we make the model more realistic? How might we simplify (or generalize) it even further?

Homework

This homework is meant to get you started creating object-oriented programs in Python.

Problem Description

Your goal is to build a piece of software for a financial institution to model one of their clients' portfolios. A portfolio can consist of 3 types of items:

- **Cash** can be added to a portfolio, removed from a portfolio or used to buy stocks/mutual funds.
- **Stock** can be purchased with existing cash in the portfolio, or sold (adding cash to the portfolio). Note that stocks can only be purchased or sold as whole units. Stocks have a price and ticker symbol. For simplicity's sake, stocks can be purchased for $X/share and when sold are sold for a price that is uniformly drawn from $[0.5\times–1.5\times]$.
- **Mutual Funds** can be purchased with existing cash in the portfolio, or sold (adding cash to the portfolio). Note that mutual funds can only be purchased as fractional shares. Mutual funds have a price and ticker symbol. For simplicity's sake, mutual funds can be purchased for $1/share and when sold are sold for a price that is uniformly drawn from $[0.9–1.2]$.

3.2 Your program must facilitate managing the correct balance of cash, stocks, and mutual funds as the user buys and sells items. Assume that the person using your library will specify the correct buy price so you can trust it and just need to maintain a proper internal state given the specified buy price (and then compute some sell price using the above formulas). Finally, in order to help with customer service your portfolio software needs to keep an audit log of all transactions and make them available to users of your program.

You can implement this software, however, you wish, but a consumer of the application must at a minimum be able to do the following:

```
# Create a new portfolio
portfolio = Portfolio()

# Add cash to the portfolio
portfolio.add_cash(300.50)

# Create Stock with price 20 and symbol "HFH"
s = Stock(20, "HFH")

# Buy 5 shares of stock s
portfolio.buy_stock(5, s)

# Create MF with symbol "BRT"
mf1 = MutualFund("BRT")

# Create MF with symbol "GHT"
mf2 = MutualFund("GHT")
```

3.3 Lab Session

```
18
19    # Buy 10.3 shares of "BRT"
20    portfolio.buy_mutual_fund(10.3, mf1)
21
22    # Buy 2 shares of "GHT"
23    portfolio.buy_mutual_fund(2, mf2)
24
25    # Display portfolio holdings
26    print(portfolio)
27    # cash: $140.50
28    # stock: 5 HFH
29    #   mutual funds: 10.33 BRT
30    #                  2       GHT
31
32    # Sell 3 shares of BRT
33    portfolio.sell_mutual_fund("BRT", 3)    \
34
35    # Sell 1 share of HFH
36    portfolio.sell_stock("HFH", 1)
37
38    # Remove $50
39    portfolio.withdraw_cash(50)
40
41    # Print a list of all transactions, ordered by time
42    portfolio.history()
```

Recommendations

Oftentimes the easiest way to work through a problem such as this is to think about what you are trying to model and assign "ownership" of data. What are the real world objects that we are dealing with? What information does each of those objects need to keep track of so that they can answer the questions required by our spec? How are these objects related and how might we make use of inheritance/polymorphism to stay DRY? What types of errors could occur?

It might be a good idea to take what we learned about TDD and see how you can apply it to this problem.

Bonus Using inheritance, show how it would be easy to add a third type of investments—Bonds—to the mix.

References

1. Heinlein, R. A. (2014). *Stranger in a strange land*. London: Hachette.
2. Schwartz, B. (2004). *The paradox of choice: Why less is more*. New York: Ecco.

Chapter 4
Introduction to Algorithms

This chapter and the next will serve as an introduction to two major topics in computer science: algorithms and data structures. Many computer science programs have a sequence of two to four courses on these topics, so our treatment here will barely scratch the surface. The purpose is not to make you an expert, but to get you thinking algorithmically.[1]

4.1 Algorithms

What are algorithms? An algorithm is a set of well-defined rules for solving a computational problem. You already use algorithms many times a day, perhaps without even thinking about it. If we take a broad view of algorithms—a series of steps that achieve a desired outcome—this could include following a recipe to prepare a meal, tying your shoes, or multiplying two matrices. For computational problems we typically care not just about what an algorithm can do, but about how fast it runs. When working on hard problems (e.g., linear programming or the analysis of large datasets) this can matter a great deal. But how do we measure the speed of an algorithm, or compare two algorithms to decide which is better? This section answers those questions within the context of sorting algorithms.

Electronic Supplementary Material The online version of this chapter (https://doi.org/10.1007/978-3-030-36826-5_4) contains supplementary material, which is available to authorized users.

[1] For a popular introduction to the influence that algorithms have had on financial trading, music, and more in the last few decades, see [2].

4.1.1 Sorting

Having an instinct for better and worse algorithms will let you know whether solving your problem will take hours or years. The task of sorting a list is a useful introduction because it is a well-understood problem and is easy to visualize.[2] Sorting also appears as a step in many more complex problems (for example, search), so a fast sorting algorithm is quite useful.

You will never have to solve the problem of sorting a list in a fast way, because programming languages like Python already have fast solutions built-in. However, there are a number of popular algorithms for sorting and learning to analyze and compare them which will help you to develop a better intuition for algorithmic complexity. It will also introduce the conceptual building blocks of more complex algorithms using methods such as "divide and conquer" (recursion) to solve computational problems.

To put this in a Python context, say we want to sort a list $[y_i, \ldots, y_n]$. What would be the *least* efficient way for us to do this? One terribly inefficient way to do this would be to randomly shuffle and then check to see if the items are in order. How many times would we expect to have to shuffle a list of length n? If $n = 1$, there is no shuffling necessary (all sorting algorithms are trivially easy for a single item). For $n = 2$ we would shuffle twice on average (or you could consider the input order to be the first shuffle). There are $n!$ ways to shuffle the list, so as the size of the input grows our expected computational effort grows factorially. In fact this is such a common way to analyze algorithms—computing the runtime in terms of the size of the input—that computer scientists have their own jargon for discussing it. We introduce this notation in the next section.

4.1.2 Computational Complexity

In computer science, we use "big-O" notation to talk about complexity. Big-O notation allows us to estimate the time required for a program to run. However, it does not use actual units of time. Rather, it is a count of the number of operations as a function of the input size.[3] That is because two different computers run the same function in different amounts of time. Furthermore, my own computer may run the same function faster or slower depending on whether I am checking email at the time (or doing any number of other things). As in many other areas, computer scientists are lazy here so they take shortcuts.

---

[2] To see nice visualizations of the sorting algorithms we discuss in this chapter and several others, visit https://www.toptal.com/developers/sorting-algorithms.

[3] Complexity analysis can also be used to discuss trade-offs in terms of memory rather than runtime, but runtime growth tends to be easier to demonstrate and therefore more natural for students developing their initial intuition for algorithmic complexity.

4.1 Algorithms

Complexity is defined mathematically. Let $|x|$ be the size of problem instance x and a be an algorithm for the problem. Suppose that for any x, the runtime $(a,x) < cf(|x|)$ for some constant c and function f. Then we say algorithm a's runtime is $O(f(|x|))$. a is polynomial-time algorithm if it is $O(f(|x|))$ for some polynomial function f. Informally, we can say that big-O notation describes the upper bound of a function's complexity.[4]

All problems that can be solved with at least one polynomial-time algorithm belong to a class called **P**. Many computer scientists consider an algorithm efficient if and only if it is polynomial time. There is another class, **NP** defined as the class of all decision problems such that if the answer is yes, there is a simple proof of that:

- The proof must have polynomial length and
- The correctness of the proof must be verifiable in polynomial time.

A problem is **NP**-hard if by supposing it is solvable in **P** implies that **P** = **NP**. Whether this is in fact true (known as the P versus NP problem) is perhaps the largest open problem in computer science.

Note that **P** means *the problem* is in polynomial time class. Your algorithm may not be in polynomial time (e.g., if it is exponential) but that an ideal answer is computable in **P** time. Computational game theorists sometimes look at whether a problem is solvable in polynomial time. If it is not, we say that it is in **NP** time.

If somebody says a problem is "in NP," that means do not waste your time trying to find a polynomial-time algorithm. (Actually they will say "NP-hard," "NP-complete," and so on—that just means someone has proven exactly which complexity class a problem belongs to.) However, just because a problem cannot be solved in polynomial time does not mean it is intractable. Many common problems—scheduling, routing, and operations on graphs (such as social networks)–cannot be solved optimally in polynomial time. Depending on the scale on which you need to operate, you may be able to find a satisfactory solution by relaxing the optimality constraint and finding an approximate answer in a reasonable amount of time. Knowing up front whether it is reasonable to seek an optimal solution or not can save you a lot of headache—and CPU cycles.

The O in big-O means $\forall\ x, f(x) < cf(x)$, and indicates how the number of computational steps grows as a function of the input size n. We drop lower-order terms and constants, so if we have a problem $n^2 + n$, we denote it $O(N^2)$ and call it "quadratic complexity." Complexity of the class $O(N)$ is called "linear" and so on. Table 4.1 lists complexity classes in increasing order. We use this notation to speak about the worst-case complexity of problems, but we can also discuss the average complexity.

---

[4]Two other notations, Ω ("big Omega") and Θ ("big Theta"), describe the lower bound and exact bounds, respectively, for a function's runtime or memory complexity. Big-O is the most common language for discussing complexity, so we focus on it here.

Table 4.1 Comparing running times

Function	Name
c	Constant
$\log N$	Logarithmic
$\log^2 N$	Log-squared
N	Linear
$N \log N$	Log-linear or linearithmic
N^2	Quadratic
N^3	Cubic
2^N	Exponential

How to Calculate Big-O

1. Assign costs to operations.

   - Each operation costs one unit (d = 4.56, d*5, etc.)
   - For loops are multiplicative: (number of statements in loop) × iterations
   - Nested for loops should be calculated from innermost loop outward
   - Consecutive statements should be added
   - If/else: calculate time for the test and add it to the maximum running time of any one branch the code might follow
   - While loops: calculate the worst-case scenario (if the loop never ends, you are in trouble because the running time is infinite)

2. Write the total cost in Big-O notation as a function of input size N (e.g., O(5))
3. Simplify:

   - Remove constants: $O(4N) \rightarrow O(N)$; $O(3N^2 + 5) \rightarrow O(N^2)$
   - Remove lower-order terms: $O(N^2 + N) \rightarrow O(N^2)$

Note that complexity is not language-specific. Big-O notation refers to the algorithm itself, not the implementation in Python, Java, or C. As an example of computing Big-O, suppose we want to compute the sum of all cubes less than n:

```
1 def sum(n):
2   partial_sum = 0 # 1 unit
3   for i in range(n+1): # n+1 units
4     partial_sum += i*i*i # 4 units
5   return partial_sum
```

The four-unit cost of computing the cubes and adding it to the partial sum occurs $n + 1$ times, for a total of $4n + 4$ times. Once we add the initial variable assignment, the running time of the function above is $O(4N + 5)$ which reduces to $O(N)$.

With this set of tools for computing, analyzing, and comparing computational complexity, we are now ready to move on to sorting algorithms. We will discuss two more sorting algorithms in addition to the "random sort" example given earlier: selection sort and merge sort.

4.1 Algorithms

Note that when we use the term "logarithmic" in this text we are using it to refer to the base-2 logarithm unless otherwise noted. This follows its conventional use by computer scientists who are accustomed to dealing with base-2 systems for binary numbers. Other languages default to base e or base 10; it is useful to check the default base when learning a new programming language.

4.1.3 Selection Sort

The key idea behind selection sort is quite simple: find the minimum value in the list and put it in the first spot, then continue putting the nth smallest item at the nth position until the list is sorted. You may have used this algorithm yourself when sorting a stack of paper or list of names, for example.

The "code" below is pseudocode, used to illustrate the algorithm rather than provide a working implementation.

Selection Sort Algorithm

```
1 k = 0, L= []
2 Loop through n-k
3     find smallest number at j
4     swap L[k] with L[j]
5     k++
```

What is the running time of selection sort? We run the sort n times to reach every item in the list, and the loop $n - k$ times. The loop runs, on average, $\frac{n+1}{2}$ times. The total runtime, then, is $\frac{n(n+1)}{2}$, for a worst-case complexity of $O(N^2)$. What about the best case (running selection sort on a pre-sorted list)? Well, we still have to check every item in the list, so it is still $O(N^2)$ (Table 4.2).

4.1.4 Merge Sort

Merge sort has two conceptual steps. First, we take the input list and split it in half again and again until it is divided into n sublists (each of size one, and thus sorted). Second, we reassemble (merge) the sublists repeatedly to create new, sorted sublists until they have all been combined into one final list.

Table 4.2 Illustrating selection sort

Round	k	j	List	Items left to check
1	0	1	[5,1,15,7,111]	5
2	1	1	[1,5,15,7,111]	4
3	2	1	[1,5,7,15,111]	3
4	3	3	[1,5,7,15,111]	

Here is a pseudocode version of merge sort:

```
1 function merge_sort(m)
2   if length(m) <= 1
3     return m
4   left = left_half_of(m)
5   right = right_half_of(m)
6   left = merge_sort(left)
7   right = merge_sort(right)
8   return merge(left, right)
```

Notice that by repeatedly splitting the input list in half, we create $\log n$ sublists (computer scientists typically use log to refer to the base-2 log). With $\log n$ split steps and n merge steps, this reduces the list sort to an $O(n \log(n))$ problem. (In this case we are not even throwing away little numbers or constants from the n.)

Try this out for yourself with an example list. It is fairly easy to sort two things and interweave them. It will take $n \log(n)$ sorts. This is true for both the best and the worst case.

4.1.5 The Economics of Algorithms

In our discussion thus far we have referred primarily to the running time of algorithms. There is another resource that we could care about too: memory. For example, merge sort takes more space than selection sort, but uses less time. Most people who care about memory work on rocket ships or microwaves. As with anything in life, there is a trade-off.

Another important distinction is between average and worst-case complexity. There is another sort, which we will not examine closely here, that most programs actually use. Quick sort is on average $O(n \log n)$, but its worst case is n^2. Again, trade-offs are important. Do not stress too much about actually computing complexity classes—they have already been computed for almost anything interesting enough that you would want to work on it. Just know how to choose between them when presented with options.

Remember that there is also a trade-off between how much time you spend programming the algorithm and how much time it will save you. In general, think about how many times you will plausibly be running the algorithm. Most working programmers look for "satisficing" solutions—fast enough and no faster.

4.2 Going Deeper

If you want to better understand the fundamental data structures and algorithms that make up an introductory computer science curriculum, we recommend [1].

4.3 Lab Session

The most important thing to point out is that algorithms are *everywhere*. An algorithm is just set-up steps that take input and produce output. Here are a couple of examples.

Boxes of macaroni and cheese (as well as many similar packaged foods) contain an algorithm for turning inputs into outputs. In this case the inputs are macaroni, powdered cheese mix, water, butter, and milk. The output is an assembled macaroni and cheese dish. Find a box on the shelf of your local supermarket (or one of the many photos available online) to answer the following questions. How many steps are involved? How much does the runtime increase if you increase the size of the outputs? If you had to "process" 100 boxes of macaroni and cheese ingredients, what techniques would you consider so that the final result did not take 100 times as long as making one box?

Another example of an algorithm that many readers will be familiar with is the process listed on bottles of shampoo. Do you notice anything wrong with this algorithm? What are its stopping conditions? If you had to write a similar process in Python what keyword would you use (is this a **for** loop or a **while** loop)? (Fig. 4.1).

At the beginning of lab, participants should be able to explain:

1. **try**
2. **except**
3. **else**
4. **finally**
5. **raise**
6. Big-Oh notation

4.3.1 Group Exercise

Go through the code for FizzBuzz as a group.[5] First, the participants should be able to explain what the implementation below does and how it works. Running `FizzBuzzLoop(16)` will raise an exception. Write a **try...except** block

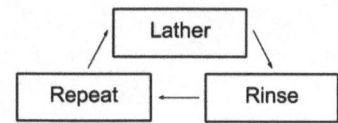

Fig. 4.1 An example of a loop: instructions on a shampoo bottle

---

[5]To understand the motivation of the FizzBuzz problem and its use in interviewing programmers, see https://blog.codinghorror.com/why-cant-programmers-program/.

to handle this error. Once you are able to handle the exception, try refactoring the
FizzBuzz function so that it prints "Fizz" and "Buzz" if the number is divisible
by 15.

fizzbuzz.py:

```
 1  def FizzBuzzLoop(upper):
 2      for i in range(1, upper):
 3          print(FizzBuzz(i))
 4
 5  def FizzBuzz(i):
 6      if i % 15 == 0:
 7          raise Exception("Divisible by both 3 and 5!")
 8      elif i % 3 == 0:
 9          return "Fizz"
10      elif i % 5 == 0:
11          return "Buzz"
12      else:
13          return i
```

4.3.2 Lab Practice

Now, have participants form groups of 2–3 to accomplish as many of the following tasks as possible with the time remaining (give them the test cases):

4.1

(a) Write an algorithm to find the square root of X. Hint: try Newton's method.[6]
(b) Find the greatest common divisor of A and B. Hint: try the Euclidean algorithm.[7]
(c) Find prime numbers up to 121 using the Sieve of Erasthones.[8]

Be sure to graph algorithmic performance. Code for this is available in the lab solutions section at the end of the book.

These exercises are meant to help illustrate the concept of recursion,[9] which is useful for this week's homework.

---

[6] http://en.wikipedia.org/wiki/Newton's_method.
[7] wikipedia.org/wiki/Euclidean_algorithm.
[8] http://en.wikipedia.org/wiki/Sieve_of_Eratosthenes.
[9] http://en.wikipedia.org/wiki/Recursion.

Homework

This homework is meant to give you feel for how different algorithms can affect runtime.

4.2 Sorting For this homework you will be required to implement two different sorting algorithms. You can choose from the ones we covered in class (not random sort) or use your own (there are lots if you spend some time searching online).

The only constraint on the two that you pick is that they must be in different complexity classes. Most likely you will need to find something that is $O(n^2)$ and $O(n \log n)$ but feel free to find something exotic or make up your own. *You must implement the sorting algorithms yourself.*

4.3 Analysis Once you have verified that your sorts are working properly (using tests), you will need to run a simulation and graph the results.

Specifically, produce a graph with the following characteristics:

- The vertical axis is some measure of time
- The horizontal axis is N (size of set to sort)
- You have one line for each sort algorithm, showing how time goes up with N
- Everything is labeled appropriately

Try to pick an N such that the effect is visually noticeable. It should not take a very large increase to make this possible.

Bonus Also graph quicksort. Note whether you are graphing average, best, or worst case runtime. To test average run times, try generating an array full of random numbers and sorting it. Do this a number of times and take the mean runtime.

References

1. Cormen, T. H., Leiserson, C. E., Rivest, R. L., & Stein, C. (2001). *Introduction to algorithms.* Cambridge: MIT Press.
2. Steiner, C. (2013). *Automate this: How algorithms took over our markets, our jobs, and the world.* New York: Portfolio.

Chapter 5
Introduction to Data Structures

Now that you are comfortable discussing algorithms and their computational complexity, it is time to introduce data structures. As we mentioned before, the two topics are often taught in tandem. This is because many of the basic methods in data structures illustrate basic algorithms, and your choice of algorithm can often be helped by employing the right data structure. Depending on our goal, a certain data structure could make our problem very simple or intractable.

Up to this point, you have primarily been using two of Python's built-in data structures: lists and dictionaries. It is natural to use these for collections of values, and they are the two most common data structures used by most Python programmers. However, there are a number of very natural applications where using these data structures will lead to poor performance. In this chapter we take a closer look at lists and dictionaries, and introduce several alternatives: queues and stacks, trees and heaps, and graphs.

To see how the choice of data structure might affect the runtime of our algorithm, look at the big-O complexity of some common methods with different data structures. Which one would be best to use if you expect to do a lot of adding and deleting but very infrequent retrieval of values? Which would be preferable if you plan to do a lot of retrieval but not much deleting? Getting a feel for how data structures work will make learning algorithms much easier.

As we discuss the use of specific data structures, it is important to think about how they are represented on your computer. Your memory, sometimes referred to as RAM, is known as the machine's "heap." When we tell the computer that an object has a certain schema, that means it allocates a certain amount of space based on how much space an object of that schema may take. In many languages, such as

---

Electronic Supplementary Material The online version of this chapter (https://doi.org/10.1007/978-3-030-36826-5_5) contains supplementary material, which is available to authorized users.

© Springer Nature Switzerland AG 2020
J. Cutler, M. Dickenson, *Computational Frameworks for Political and Social Research with Python*, Textbooks on Political Analysis,
https://doi.org/10.1007/978-3-030-36826-5_5

Java, at the time that you create an object you must indicate how much memory it requires. Python is less rigid about this, which makes it easier for beginners but also obfuscates some of the details of underlying data structures. When Python differs substantially from lower-level languages we will indicate it below, but we can still use it to illustrate the same concepts.

5.1 Arrays and Lists

An array is a collection of items selected by index. We define an array in Python with something like a = [1, 2, "a"]. When you do this, your computer gives the object a exactly three spaces (an imprecise term for the moment) of memory. We can index these things quickly because we are keeping track. However, the trade-off is that adding something to the list is costly, because the amount of memory it is allocated must be increased.

Lists are arrays that do not allow direct indexing. Rather than allocating a block of memory, a list is stored as items that each point to the next item in the list. Each element in the list is referred to as a *node* which has *data* and a *pointer* to the next node. The only way to get the second thing out of memory is to get the first thing out of memory and ask it where the second thing is hiding. If we want the fourth (or the nth element, that can require a lot of asking. To find something, we have to use a search algorithm, typically starting at the middle and working our way out. Notice that it would be much easier to find items if the list were sorted.

The benefit of a list is that you can add things to it indefinitely. Furthermore, they can grow indefinitely as well because Python does not allocate a fixed space for the list when it was created. For your homework you will be creating a list of this type in Python.

The following example shows the difference in behavior between arrays and lists in Python.

```
1  import sys
2
3  from array import array
4
5  # initialize an array
6  my_array = array('i', [1, 2, 3])
7  print(my_array[0])
8  print(id(my_array))
9
10 # change a value
11 my_array[0] = 0
12 print(id(my_array))
13
14 # check memory size
```

```
15  print(sys.getsizeof(my_array))
16
17  # initialize a list
18  my_list = [1, 2, 3]
19
20  # check memory size
21  print(sys.getsizeof(my_list))
22
23  # change a value to a different type
24  my_list[0] = 'abc'
25
26  # check memory size again
27  print(sys.getsizeof(my_list))
```

The first thing to notice is that Python makes it easy to use lists by not requiring them to be imported. Arrays, however, must be imported from Python's `array` module. As you start to work with more advanced data structures it will be common to import them either from Python's standard library (modules that are included by default when you install Python) or third-party modules such as NumPy.

The second difference you can see is that when we initialize an array we must indicate which type of values we plan to store in it. In this case, `'i'` indicates that we will use integers. With lists, though, we can mix values of any type.

The final important thing to notice is the difference in the amount of memory each collection occupies. Storing three integers in an array only takes up 68 bytes (the return value of `sys.getsizeof()`), while storing three integers in a list takes 96 bytes. The additional memory overhead that the list requires is the cost of its flexibility—because it is easy to combine values of different types, Python must allocate enough memory to handle larger objects even if we are not using them when we initialize the list.

If you are choosing between arrays and lists in Python, you should use lists unless you have a very good reason to choose arrays (for example, you have already verified the correctness of your code and are trying to squeeze out performance optimizations in an operation that must be run many, many times).

5.2 Queues and Stacks

Queues and stacks are more specialized data structures, usually built with a list or array underneath. Data structures are often cumulative in this way, with some structures being special cases of others. The ability to compose complex data structures out of simpler pieces should remind you of the way that we composed sorting algorithms out of smaller subroutines in the previous chapter.

Table 5.1 Running time for common operations in various data structures

Method	Arrays	Lists	Queues/Stacks	Dictionary	Trees
Add	$O(1)$ or $O(n)$	$O(1)$	$O(1)$	$O(1)$	$O(\log n)$
Delete	$O(n)$	$O(1)$	$O(1)$	$O(1)$	$O(\log n)$
Find	$O(n)$	$O(n)$	$O(n)$	$O(n)$	$O(\log n)$

Visualize a queue like a line at the airport (in fact speakers of British English are more likely to call these queues than lines).[1] There are only two possible operations: adding something to the end of the queue ("enqueueing") or removing it from the front of the queue ("dequeueing"). Put differently, we have no other access to the items in our queue other than in a first-in-first-out (FIFO) manner. Given that we are only adding and deleting items from the collection, which data structure would you prefer for implementing a queue?

Hopefully you said a list, because we are not going to be doing searching, just adding and deleting. Review Table 5.1 if you made a different choice. Queues are not available in Python unless you import them from the standard library (the queue module in Python 3, which was renamed from Queue in Python 2), but you could also implement one yourself if you are so inclined.

A closely related data structure is stacks. As the name would suggest, this can be best visualized as a stack of things, such as a deck of cards. When you add something, it is added to the end (or top, if you are using a visual metaphor) and you remove items from the end. This is the last-in-first-out (LIFO) method.

When we add to a stack we call it "pushing" and when we remove something we call it "popping." Python supports these operations natively. As with lists and arrays, Python conflates the difference between stacks and queues (the deque data structure in the collections module supports the behavior of both queues and stacks). If you are working with data of known size, this is not a huge problem.

Notice that stacks are the data structure referred to in "stack traces" (which came up in our discussion of exceptions) and "stack overflows" (the origin of the name for the useful help site, http://stackoverflow.com). Your computer uses a stack to manage the operations that being executed.

In the pseudocode below, the user calls a, which in turn calls b, which in turn calls c and returns one. How does something get popped off? A function is popped off when it returns. A recursive function just puts itself on the stack over and over again. Fortunately, Python tries to help you (in the terminal at least) by keeping you from overflowing the stack with recursive functions.

```
>>> def a():
...         return b()
...
```

---

[1] You might recall that in the early days of Netflix, customers could set up a "queue" of items that they wanted to view. This was a very natural term for the programmers who were developing Netflix, but many American customers were unfamiliar with the term and it was eventually changed to "watchlist."

5.4 Trees and Heaps

```
>>> def b():
...     return c()
>>>
>>> def c():
...     return 1
>>>
>>> a()
... 1
```

When an exception occurs, the stack trace is returned, which will tell you all of the functions that failed to catch it. Because a CPU core only does one thing at a time, a stack is an efficient way to handle it. An eight-core computer has eight stacks.

5.3 Dictionaries and Hashtables

Dictionaries take their name from their resemblance to a certain type of reference book (no surprise). In a conventional printed dictionary the key is the word and the value stored at that location is the definition. But you can make much more flexible dictionaries with Python. For example, you can make the key a letter and its value the number of times that letter appears in a certain sentence.

Dictionaries provide a quick lookup for arbitrary things. They sometimes go by the name "hashtables" because they use a hash function to assign a unique identifier (typically a number) to the object that the arbitrary key should point to.

```
>>> a = {}
>>> a["foo"] = "bar"
```

When we run the above code, we tell the computer a + 'foo' = memory location. The pointer that gets us from input to output is the hash function. The main point here is that you should not be doing a lot of searching through a dictionary, because it is bad for that. What dictionaries are good for is adding and removing a lot of things very quickly, and to access them (but not sort them). This is one of the most commonly used data structures for a reason: it is great for when you do not know how many data points you will have, but you want to get to them quickly. Understanding lists and dictionaries are the most important points in this chapter.

5.4 Trees and Heaps

Trees come in many shapes, but it is easiest to visualize a binary tree (think game theory; each node has at most two branches). The nodes of the tree are stored with pointers to the other items. In a binary tree, each node points to its right and left "child" (which may be empty if the node is a leaf). The top is the "root," anything that does not have another node after it is a "leaf." The distance between any node and the root is called the "depth" of the node and the depth of the farthest leaf is the height of the tree (yes, computer scientists have been known to mix metaphors).

Depending on the properties you enforce for your tree, you can get interesting patterns. If you put numbers into your tree in a certain way, you can access them very quickly. One special implementation is a binary search tree: everything to the right has a greater value than its parent node, everything to the left is smaller than its parent node. This makes searching the tree an O(log n) operation, which can be a great time-saver.

You can think of a list as a degenerate case of a tree. Trees are pretty easy to create, so many people make their own. Trees can also be used to implement heaps, where the order of sorting can be smallest-to-largest ("min heap") or largest-to-smallest ("max heap").[2]

Imagine a min heap, in which the parent has to be less than its two children. When we add an item to the heap, we have to have a special operation to make sure it goes into the right spot. This means that accessing items is quick but adding them can be more time-consuming than with other structures. However, we get a benefit from knowing the order in which items will be returned. Heaps can also be stored in arrays, with the parent node at index n and its children at $2n$ and $2n+1$ (we usually skip zero). This allows us to easily go back and forth between parents and children.

Suppose you are looking for the fourth smallest element in a min heap. It cannot be at the root because that is the smallest. This means there cannot possibly be four smaller elements above it. That means it could be anywhere on the second or third level: anywhere from indexes 2–15 (Fig. 5.1).

A heap goes through each level of the tree and puts those things into an array. So a hierarchy of 1–7 in the conventional fashion (1 is parent of 2 and 3, 2 is parent of 4 and 5) would be stored as an array of (null, 1,2,3,4,5,6,7). If you tried to add a node that was equal to another node it would bubble up until it hit its parent or its grandparent, depending on how you defined it.

Fig. 5.1 Hierarchical heap structure

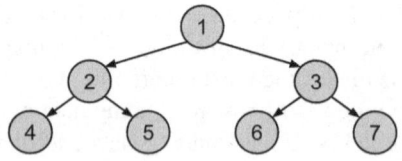

---

[2] We can also assign "importance" or "priority" to objects and store them in a heap, known as a "priority queue." However, this is beyond the scope of this chapter.

5.5 Graphs

If you conduct a survey of computer scientists, graphs would probably win out as the favorite data structure. They consist of nodes (also known as "vertices") and edges to connect them. Nodes are used to hold your data (or nothing at all, if you prefer). Edges are defined in pairs of vertices. For example, the edge (1,2) connects nodes 1 and 2. If the edges are *directed*, then 1 "points to" 2 and (2,1) is not the same as (1,2). We typically abbreviate "directed graph" to "digraph." In an undirected graph, the edges (1,2) and (2,1) are equivalent.

Another feature of a graph is that the edges can have *weights*. For example, the cost of traveling between 1 and 2 could be 3. Think of this as the distance between cities, the cost of a phone call, or a similar metric. Weighted edges are interesting in the traveling salesman problem (an NP-hard problem). In this problem, the edges are weighted by the mileage between the cities. Edges can be directed or non-directed, which governs how the graph can be traversed. A graph is "cyclic" if you can get back to your starting point for any smaller portion of the graph.

To make things more confusing, people like to abbreviate graph terminology. A DAG is a Directed Acyclic Graph. Directional means that the edge (A, B) is distinct from the edge (B, A), and acyclic means that there is no way to end up at the same node where you started traversing the graph. Trees can be thought of as degenerate cases of graphs, and are by definition DAGs. Graphs can also be represented using an adjacency matrix, where the cell (i, j) takes the weight of the edge from node i to node j, or just 1's and 0's for unweighted graphs (also known as a binary matrix). Note that if your graph is undirected, using a matrix will result in redundant information since the entry (i, j) must be equal to the entry (j, i).

The graph illustrated in Fig. 5.2 has three nodes and three edges. The nodes are labeled "A," "B," and "C." The edges are from A to B (weight three), A to C (weight two), and B to C (weight one). Note that this is an abstract representation that could be used to describe a wide variety of underlying situations: three websites with varying numbers of links to one another, three employees at a firm who send different numbers of messages, or three cities with travel distances between them. Graphs are a very flexible representation, but often a more restrictive structure such as a list or tree is sufficiently expressive for a given task.

Fig. 5.2 Example of a directed acyclic graph

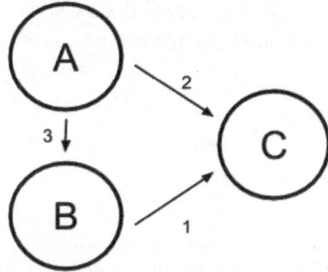

Graphs are not terribly common in Python, but you will get practice with them in the lab session. We will use a simple representation of a graph as a nested dictionary. The first level of keys is the nodes. The next level is the nodes to which that node is a neighbor. The final level of the dictionary (the innermost value) could be either a weight, or a fixed value such as one for an unweighted graph.

To represent the graph in the figure above using a dictionary, we could set it up as follows:

```
{
  "A": {
    "B": 3,
    "C": 2
  },
  "B": {
    "C": 1
  },
  "C": {}
}
```

The lab session will show you how to work with a graph stored as a dictionary, including setting up helper functions for your convenience.

5.6 Lab Session

Chain networks and ring networks are special types of graphs. In a chain network, each node has an edge to its two neighbors, and they are arranged in a linear fashion (like houses on a street). In a ring network, the beginning and end nodes of the chain are connected (like houses in a cul-de-sac). As you can guess, a grid network is set up so that each node points to its four (N, S, E, W) or eight (N, NE, E, SE, S, SW, W, NW) neighbors.

In the starter code below you have been given some functions to create graphs. The `make_link()` function takes a graph and adds an edge between two nodes (and can add the nodes themselves if needed).[3] On lines 14–20 of the code below we create a ring network using a **for** loop. How many nodes should this ring have? How many edges?

After reviewing this starter code, have participants join in groups of 2–3 and complete the following exercises (listed as TODO statements in the code):

---

[3] This code is based in part on [1] and in part on an exercise from Udacity's CS 215 course.

5.1

(a) Use the code to count how many edges a 16×16 grid network would have.
(b) Play around with the movie graph (or another graph of your choosing). Lots of information about actors' linkages can be found here. Can you find an Eulerian tour of the movie graph? Who does it end with? Verify your answer in Python.[4]
(c) Implement `findShortestPath` and `findAllPaths` based on the code given for `findPath`.

The following script helps to demonstrate recursion:

```
 1 def factorial(x):
 2     if x <= 1: # base case
 3         val = 1
 4     else: # recursive case
 5         val = x*factorial(x-1)
 6     return val
 7
 8 print(factorial(1))
 9 print(factorial(2))
10 print(factorial(3))
11 print(factorial(6))
```

If there is not time to finish all of these tasks in lab that is fine—just do as many as you can. Note that recursion is the key to completing all of these algorithms (there are other ways, but we want you to learn recursion for the homework assignment).

Discuss the Big-Oh complexity of each algorithm.

algs.py:

```
 1 """Working with Graphs/Networks"""
 2
 3 def make_link(G, node1, node2):
 4     if node1 not in G:
 5         G[node1] = {}
 6     G[node1][node2] = 1
 7     if node2 not in G:
 8         G[node2] = {}
 9     G[node2][node1] = 1
10     return G
11
12 # Ring Network
13 ring = {} # empty graph
14
15 n = 5 # number of nodes
16
```

---

[4]Eulerian path.

```python
17  # Add in edges
18  for i in range(n):
19      ring = make_link(ring, i, (i+1)%n)
20
21  # How many nodes?
22  print(len(ring))
23
24  # Grid Network
25  # TODO: create a square graph with 256 nodes and count
        the edges
26  # TODO: define a function count_edges
27
28  # Social Network
29  class Actor(object):
30      def __init__(self, name):
31          self.name = name
32
33      def __repr__(self):
34          return self.name
35
36  ss = Actor("Susan Sarandon")
37  jr = Actor("Julia Roberts")
38  kb = Actor("Kevin Bacon")
39  ah = Actor("Anne Hathaway")
40  rd = Actor("Robert DiNero")
41  ms = Actor("Meryl Streep")
42  dh = Actor("Dustin Hoffman")
43
44  movies = {}
45
46  make_link(movies, dh, rd)  # Wag the Dog
47  make_link(movies, rd, ms)  # Marvin's Room
48  make_link(movies, dh, ss)  # Midnight Mile
49  make_link(movies, dh, jr)  # Hook
50  make_link(movies, dh, kb)  # Sleepers
51  make_link(movies, ss, jr)  # Stepmom
52  make_link(movies, kb, jr)  # Flatliners
53  make_link(movies, kb, ms)  # The River Wild
54  make_link(movies, ah, ms)  # Devil Wears Prada
55  make_link(movies, ah, jr)  # Valentine's Day
56
57  # How many nodes in movies?
58  # How many edges in movies?
59
```

```
60  def tour(graph, nodes):
61      for ix, node in enumerate(nodes):
62          if node in graph.keys():
63              print(node)
64          else:
65              print("Node not found!")
66              break
67          if ix+1 < len(nodes):
68              next_node = nodes[ix+1]
69              if next_node in graph.keys():
70                  if next_node in graph[node].keys():
71                      pass
72                  else:
73                      print("Can't get there from here!")
74                      break
75
76  # TODO: find an Eulerian tour of the movie network and
    check it
77  movie_tour = []
78  tour(movies, movie_tour)
79
80
81  def find_path(graph, start, end, path=None):
82      if path is None:
83          path = []
84      path = path + [start]
85      if start == end:
86          return path
87      if start not in graph:
88          return None
89      for node in graph[start]:
90          if node not in path:
91              newpath = find_path(graph, node, end, path)
92              if newpath:
93                  return newpath
94      return None
95
96  print(find_path(movies, jr, ms))
97
98
99  # TODO: implement find_shortest_path()
100 # print find_shortest_path(movies, ms, ss)
101
```

```
102 # TODO: implement find_all_paths() to find all paths
          between two nodes
103 # all_paths = find_all_paths(movies, jr, ms)
104 # for path in all_paths:
105 #     print path
```

Homework

This homework is meant to guide you through implementing a data structure. For this homework you will be implementing a linked list. Note that this is a very common problem and you will be able to find the solutions readily on the Internet. Try not to.

Singly Linked List

A Singly Linked List is a list comprised of many nodes. Each node contains some data, in our case just an integer, and a pointer to the next node in the list. The first node in the list is known as the *head* node. The last node in the graph has a pointer to a *null* next item. Represented graphically, a Singly Linked List looks like this (note that the *head* has value 5 and the *tail* has value 2):

Your assignment is to implement a LinkedList class with the following interface:

- `__init__(self, value)`: Takes a number and sets it as the value at the head of the List
- `length(self)`: Returns the length of the list
- `add_node(self, new_value)`: Takes a number and adds it to the end of the list
- `add_node_fter(self, new_value, after_node)`: Takes a number and adds it after the *after_node*
- `add_node_before(self, new_value, before_node)`: Takes a value and adds before the *before_node*
- `remove_node(self, node_to_remove)`: Removes a node from the list
- `remove_nodes_by_value(self, value)`: Takes a value, removes all nodes with that value
- `reverse(self)`: Reverses the order of the linked list
- `__str__(self)__`: Displays the list in some reasonable way
- `has_cycle(self)`: Bonus: Returns true if this linked list has a cycle. This is non-trivial

For each of the above methods, figure out what the computation complexity of your implementation is and state whether or not you think that is the best possible complexity class. Make sure that your implementation is correct and robust to bad inputs.

You are free to define whatever private helper functions/classes/etc. that you need, but make sure that your implementation has the above public facing interface. You may NOT use any other data structures to implement this. That means no Lists, Arrays, Tuples, etc. You should use the following as the starter definition for a Node class:

```
class Node(object):

    def __init__(self, _value=None, _next=None):
        self.value = _value
        self.next = _next

    def __str__(self):
        return str(self.value)
```

Reference

1. Downey, A. (1991). *Think python.* Sebastopol: O'Reilly.

Chapter 6
Input, Output, and the Web

With our discussion of algorithms and data structures completed, we are finished with the computer science portion of the book and move into programming. This means that we are moving on to practical software development, and no longer discussing algorithms and complexity for their own sake.

The most important lesson to remember from the previous chapters is that as your problem gets big, the details of your implementation become very important. Differences in running time that are imperceptible at an input size of 10 can become quite painful when the input grows to ten million. Algorithms are all about speed. For historical reasons, there is an important assumption built into most algorithms: that reading and writing to the disk is slow. In this chapter we will look at the process of reading and writing data, otherwise known as input–output (I/O).

6.1 Disks

Most algorithms are optimized not only by reducing the number of operations, but by minimizing the amount of reading from and writing to a disk (usually the hard drive of a single computer). This is because the slowest part of a computer is the hard drive. The hard drive is the only real mechanical part on a modern computer. While everything else in your computer happens at the speed of light (or at least at that order of magnitude), a hard drive spins at 5400 or 7200 rpm. This is why the hard drive is often the first part of a computer to fail. Hardware improvements such as increased availability of solid-state drives (SSDs) will reduce the relevance

---

Electronic Supplementary Material The online version of this chapter (https://doi.org/10.1007/978-3-030-36826-5_6) contains supplementary material, which is available to authorized users.

Table 6.1 Latency for common operations in milliseconds

Operation	Time (ms)
Read 1 MB from memory (RAM)	0.25
Read 1 MB from SSD	1
Read 1 MB from disk	20

of this section, but for now they are not widespread enough that we can ignore the time costs of reading from and writing to the hard disk.

6.2 The Cost of Input and Output

As shown in Table 6.1, reading from disk takes about 80 times as long as reading the same amount of data from the random access memory (RAM). This is why statistical analyses of a scale typical for social science research often involve loading the data into memory once, performing a series of transformations and modeling exercises, and then producing output. If your data fit into memory your program will be able to run much faster than if it involves reading from disk repeatedly.

Other input and output operations are similarly costly. If your program prints a running log of its operations, that introduces overhead. One popular package management tool for Javascript, npm, was once two to four times slower if it was run with an option to display a progress toolbar.[1]

Fetching data over the Internet is even more costly. At the theoretical limit (i.e., the speed of light in a vacuum), it would take 40 ms for one bit of information to make a round trip between Paris and New York. In reality, packets transferring across the Internet are almost never able to travel in a straight line for such long distances, so actual times are much slower.[2] High latency numbers like these make such a difference to high-frequency trading firms that billions of dollars have been invested in reducing the round-trip time for data between Chicago and New York from 14.5 ms (1000 mile path) to 8.5 ms (731 mile path; this is a little over twice the theoretical lower bound of 3.9 ms) [1].

6.3 Writing to the Disk in Python

File I/O is mainly about *streams*. One important stream you already know about is stdout ("standard out"): this is where output goes when you call **print** in Python. Another important stream is stdin, which you get by calling

---

[1] See https://github.com/npm/npm/issues/11283.
[2] Readers familiar with the R statistical programming environment will recall the option to choose which CRAN mirror to use for installing packages, in large part to reduce latency.

6.3 Writing to the Disk in Python

`raw_input()`. Knowing how to manipulate these two streams allows you to write a large number of programs.

A data stream is a source from which you can pull data indefinitely. One way to think of it is as a list with an unknown length. The elements of the stream could be anything from individual bits to packets in a file you are downloading over the Internet.

When working with data streams, we can read as little data at a time as we want, down to a single bit. However, when dealing with text files (for example), a single bit does not carry much meaning. We typically prefer to read chunks of the file in bytes. One byte consists of eight bits; typical file sizes are measured in kilobytes (1024 bytes), megabytes (1024 kilobytes), and so on. For most encoding schemes, a byte is enough to represent one character of text.

To accomplish the reading of one byte at a time I/O, we use *buffers*. Buffering specifies how much of the input to read in at each step. One of the most useful buffers for dealing with data is the line buffer—we are able to tell Python to read in the file one line at a time.

You can see the use of different buffer sizes in the following code. (The contents of `readfile.txt` here are not important, but if you want to run the example code yourself you could create a text file with the contents of your departmental web page, for example.)

filestuff.py:

```
1  import os
2  import sys
3
4  with open('readfile.txt', 'w') as f:
5      f.write(str(os.urandom(1024)))
6
7  # The cleanest way to handle files (gracefully handles
       exceptions)
8  with open('readfile.txt') as f:
9      #We can read files in chunks
10     the_whole_thing = f.read()
11     print("The Whole
       Thing\n********\n{0}".format(the_whole_thing))
12
13     # We can read files line by line
14     print("\nLooping over lines\n********\n")
15     f.seek(0)
16     lines = f.readlines()
17     for l in lines:
18         print("{0}".format(l))
19
```

```
20      # More efficiently we can loop over the file object
21      # (i.e. we don't need the variable lines)
22      print("\nLooping over the file
        object\n*********\n")
23      f.seek(0)
24      for l in f:
25          print("{0}".format(l))
26
27      #You can also go byte by byte (don't do this)
28      print("\nByte by Byte\n********\n")
29      f.seek(0)
30      next_byte = f.read(1)
31      while next_byte != "":
32          sys.stdout.write(next_byte)
33          next_byte = f.read(1)
34
35 # We can also manually open and close files,
36 # But now we need to handle exceptions and closing
        files
37 f = open('readfile.txt')
38 print("\nManually Opened File\n********\n")
39 print(f.read())
40 f.close()
41
42 #Writing files is easy, too
43 with open('writefile.txt', 'w') as f:
44      #wipes the file clean and opens it
45      f.write("Hi guys.")
46      f.write("Does this go on the second line?")
47      f.writelines(['a', 'b', 'c'])
48      # If using the file object interactively you may
        need to flush the buffer
49      # f.flush()
50
51 with open('writefile.txt', 'a') as f:
52      # just tacks content onto the end of the file
53      f.write("\nI got appended!")
54      f.flush()
```

First, we open the file and give it the alias of f. Calling f.read() loads the entire contents of the file at once. Note that this is a risky operation if you do not know the size of the file, since it might be larger than what your computer can hold in memory.

After reading the whole file, our pointer to its contents is at the end of the file. To get back to the beginning, we call f.seek(0) to move the pointer back to the 0th

6.3 Writing to the Disk in Python

byte of the file—the very beginning of the stream. Next, we read the file line by line with `f.readlines()` and iterate over them.

A third way of iterating over the file is byte by byte (lines 23–28). This is generally not a good idea, both because individual bytes carry very little meaning and because if you do not know the encoding of the file then it is not worth reading a byte at a time.

We can also write to files by opening them with the "w" option ("write") instead of "r" ("read"). Notice that this will destroy any contents of the file if it already exists. If you want to append onto the end of a file, you can use the "a" option ("append").

6.3.1 CSV Files

You can work with CSV files—a common and easily transferable data format—in a similar way, using the `csv` library:

csvstuff.py:

```
1  import csv
2
3  # Open a file stream and create a CSV writer object
4  f = open('test.csv', 'w')
5  my_writer = csv.writer(f)
6
7  for i in range(1, 100):
8      my_writer.writerow([i, i-1])
9
10 f.flush()
11 f.close()
12
13 # The correct way!
14 with open('test1.csv', 'w') as f:
15     my_writer = csv.writer(f)
16     for i in range(1, 100):
17         my_writer.writerow([i, i-1])
18
19 # How about with field names
20 with open('test_with_fields.csv', 'w') as f:
21     my_writer = csv.DictWriter(f, fieldnames=("A", "B"))
22     my_writer.writeheader()
23     for i in range(1, 100):
24         my_writer.writerow({"B":i, "A":i-1})
25
```

```
26  # Now lets read some things
27  with open('test1.csv', 'r') as f:
28      print("Reading test1.csv")
29      my_reader = csv.reader(f)
30      for row in my_reader:
31          print(row)
32
33  #Now lets read some things with field names
34  with open('test_with_fields.csv', 'r') as f:
35      print("\nReading test_with_fields.csv")
36      my_reader = csv.DictReader(f)
37      for row in my_reader:
38          print(row)
```

This example code shows a variety of ways to access CSV data. First, we import the `csv` module from Python's standard library. We then set up a `writer` that will accept data one row at a time. Calling the `writerow` function with a list of elements writes the list as a comma-separated row. If you wanted to set up a header row in the file with column names, you could do that as the first line. We then call `flush` to ensure that all of our data has been written before closing the file.

Notice one downside of this first approach: we had to remember to `close` the file when we were done. If we had encountered an error before closing, we might have left the file in a bad state (such as a partially written row). A better way to do this in Python is to use a context handler. The second example (starting on line 14) does this. We open the file and give it an alias of `f`. By using a context manager, Python takes care of closing the file gracefully when we are done (or if the code encounters an error).

The third example (line 20) shows how to use `DictWriter` to write each row as a dictionary. This format is nice if you have a large number of columns, since you do not have to worry about the order of the elements in the list as you write to each row.

Similarly, you can use `reader` to read rows as lists and `DictReader` to read rows as dictionaries. Both ways of accessing CSV data work well, and your choice will often depend on how you plan to work with the data after reading it.

6.4 HTML and HTTP

With CSVs we saw Python's ability to handle files that were in a known format. Similarly, every HTML (Hypertext Markup Language) document on the web is structured in a particular way. Think of HTML as a contract for how you should structure the document so the web browser knows what to draw on the screen. Our discussion will refer to HTML as it should be. This is an ideal that does not exist on 99% of the web. Fortunately, because this is such a common problem, there are a number of useful libraries that help "clean up" HTML into easily processed data (Table 6.2).

6.4 HTML and HTTP

Table 6.2 Common HTML tags

Tag	Name	Usage
`<a>`	Anchor	Hyperlinks
`<b>`	Bold	Show text in bold
`<div>`	Divider	Define a section of a document
`<i>`	Italics	Emphasize text with italics
`<img>`	Image	Display an image
`<li>`	List item	Item in an `<ol>` or `<ul>` list
`<ol>`	Ordered list	List with automatic numbering
`<span>`	Span	Organize a line of content
`<table>`	Table	Tabular data
`<th>`	Table header	First row of a table
`<td>`	Table data	Cell of a table
`<tr>`	Table row	Row of a table (contains cells)
`<ul>`	Unordered list	Display a bulleted list of items

Here is an example of HTML and what it allows you to do:

```
1 <thing>
2   <nested_thing>
3
4   </nested_thing>
5 </thing>
```

Essentially, all HTML is just items with nested sub-items, with their own sub-sub-items, and so on. Each item type is denoted by the < > tags, but the identifiers inside those tags are arbitrary. You can view real-world HTML documents by going to any web page in a browser, right-clicking, and selecting "view page source".

Here is a stylized example of a web page:

```
1  <html>
2    <head>          # not visible
3      <title>Page Title</title>
4    </head>
5
6    <body>
7      <h1>Foo</h1> # a header block (headers go from h1
         to h6,
8  decreasing in size)
9      <p>bar</p>    # a paragraph tag
10     <a href="google.com">google</a> # a hyperlink
11     <img src = "pic.png"> # an image
12     <div>         # a divider
13     <table>       # care to guess?
14     <span>
15     <hr>
```

```
16
17     </body>
18 </html>
```

Because nice, clean HTML like this is so rare, libraries for parsing HTML are available in almost every language. A good one in Python is BeautifulSoup. Note that the pip install bs4 step is meant to be run in your shell (command line), not in the Python console.

url_grabbing.py:

```
1  # First install BeautifulSoup: pip install bs4
2  from bs4 import BeautifulSoup
3  from urllib.request import urlopen
4
5
6  # Open a webpage
7  webpage = urlopen('https://polisci.duke.edu/graduate')
8  # Parse it
9  soup = BeautifulSoup(webpage.read(), features="lxml")
10
11 #Print out the target destinations for the links
12 print("Links\n*******************")
13 for link in soup('a'):
14     if 'href' in link:
15         print(str(link['href']))
16
17 print("Headers\n*******************")
18 for header in soup(['h1', 'h2', 'h3']):
19     print("{0}: {1}".format(header.name,
       header.string))
20
21 #Crawl the next 3 links?
```

In this example we use another library (urllib2) to download the web page itself. Think of this as just another stream. The basic HTTP (HyperText Transfer Protocol) has four main operations: GET, POST, PUT, and DELETE. (See the following chapter for more details about HTTP requests.) When you use urllib2 to open a page, you are issuing a GET request. With all of these acronyms, you can probably see where BeautifulSoup gets its name. We will get into more detail about HTML and HTTP in the next chapter.

Because the contract of structured web pages exists, we were easily able to find the links on the example page. Think about how you would recursively use this to crawl an entire website. However, before you start crawling everything, keep in mind a few more norms of the web. If a site has a sitemap.xml, that will tell you what to index. If it has a robots.txt file, that tells you what not to index. And if a tag indicates rel="nofollow", your web crawler should not go there. Keep in mind that your laptop doing an automated crawl is much faster than the way people normally use the Internet. Use a delay so that you do not cause problems for the website that you are crawling—1 or 2 s will suffice.

With these tools and guidelines in place, along with the searching method you will learn in the lab section, you are prepared to start scraping the web for data.

6.5 Lab Session

Discuss the following concepts and commands, making sure everyone understands them before proceeding with the lab:

- loops
- accessing a web page
- clean_html
- re.search()
- opening and closing a CSV

6.5.1 Regular Expressions

To efficiently search and process text, we will use regular expressions, or "regex." Regular expressions are available in most programming languages and it is helpful to know a bit about them because they are extremely fast.

The Python documentation has a helpful guide on regex but it is a little complicated for beginners.[3] The main things to take away from it are the explanation of metacharacters and:

- \d Matches any decimal digit; this is equivalent to the class [0-9].
- \D Matches any non-digit character; this is equivalent to the class [^0-9].
- \s Matches any whitespace character; this is equivalent to the class [\t\n\r\f\v].
- \S Matches any non-whitespace character; this is equivalent to the class [^\t\n\r\f\v].
- \w Matches any alphanumeric character; this is equivalent to the class [a-zA-Z0-9_].
- \W Matches any non-alphanumeric character; this is equivalent to the class [^a-zA-Z0-9_]

Another useful list of regex usage is adapted from http://www.upriss.org.uk/python/session7.html:

- . Any single character except a newline
- ^ The beginning of the line or string

---

[3]http://docs.python.org/2/howto/regex.html.

- $ The end of the line or string
- * Zero or more of the last character
- + One or more of the last character
- ? Zero or one of the last character
- {5,10} Five to ten times the previous character

If you want to practice more with regular expressions in Python, check out PyRegex,[4] and if you want to get better at regular expressions in general you might enjoy Regex Crossword.[5]

6.1 Download a plain-text file from bit.ly/obama2008nh and save it as `obama-nh.txt` in the same directory where you are launching the Python interpreter.[6] Use the following example and complete the challenges to get better with regular expressions:

`regexp.py`:

```
1  import re
2
3  # open text file of 2008 NH primary Obama speech
4  f = open("obama-nh.txt", "r")
5  text = f.readlines()
6  f.close()
7
8  # compile the regular expression
9  keyword = re.compile(r"the ")
10
11 # search file for keyword, line by line
12 for line in text:
13     if keyword.search(line):
14         print(line)
15
16 # TODO: print all lines that DO NOT contain "the "
17 # TODO: print lines that contain a word of any length
       starting with s and ending with e
18
19 # date = raw_input("Please enter a date in the format
       MM.DD.YY: ")
20 # keyword = re.compile(r"(\d\d?)\.(\d\d?)\.(\d\d)")
21 # result = keyword.search(date)
22 # if result:
23 #     print("Month: ", result.group(1))
```

---

[4]http://www.pyregex.com/.
[5]https://regexcrossword.com/.
[6]As the name suggests, this file contains Barack Obama's 2008 New Hampshire primary speech.

```
24 #    print("Day: ", result.group(2))
25 #    print("Year: ", result.group(3))
26
27 # TODO: Write a regular expression that finds html
        tags in example.html and prints them.
```

6.5.2 Web Scraping

Now that you know how to search text with regular expressions, you can put them to work for web scraping purposes. As an example, we will look at the White House petitions page. As a fun aside, the White House petition site (https://petitions.whitehouse.gov/petitions) is actually open source.[7] By reading a few of their files on Github you can get a better idea for how the site is structured.

6.2 Play around with the following file to get data of interest to you from the petitions site:

scraping.py:

```
1  # Scraper to collect petition info from
       petitions.whitehouse.gov
2
3  import csv
4
5  from bs4 import BeautifulSoup
6  from urllib.request import urlopen
7
8  # What page?
9  page_to_scrape = 'https://petitions.whitehouse.gov/'
10
11 # What info do we want?
12 headers = ["Summary", "Signatures"]
13
14 # Where do we save info?
15 filename = "whitehouse-petitions.csv"
16 with open(filename, "w") as readFile:
17     csvwriter = csv.writer(readFile)
18     csvwriter.writerow(headers)
19
20 # Open webpage
21 webpage = urlopen(page_to_scrape)
```

---

[7] https://github.com/WhiteHouse/petitions.

```
22
23  # Parse it
24  soup = BeautifulSoup(webpage.read())
25  soup.prettify()
26
27  # Extract petitions on page
28  petitions = soup.findAll("h3")
29  print(len(petitions))
30  for petition in petitions:
31      link = petition.find("a")
32      if link is None:
33         continue
34      p = link.get_text()
35      print(p)
36
37  signatures = soup.findAll("div",
        attrs={'class':'signatures-progress-bar'})
38  print(len(signatures))
39  for signature in signatures:
40      signature_num = signature.find("span",
        attrs={'class':'signatures-number'})
41      if signature_num is None:
42         continue
43      s = signature_num.get_text()
44      print(s)
45
46  with open(filename, "w") as readFile:
47      csvwriter = csv.writer(readFile)
48      for i in range(len(signatures)):
49          petition = petitions[i]
50          p = petition.find("a")
51          if p is None:
52             continue
53          signature = signatures[i]
54          s = signature.find("span",
        attrs={'class':'signatures-number'})
55          if s is None:
56             continue
57
        csvwriter.writerow([p.get_text().encode('ascii',
        'ignore'), s.get_text().encode('ascii', 'ignore')])
```

Homework

This homework is designed to get you thinking about how to implement a web crawler.

Pick your favorite (small) blog, e.g. chrisblattman.com or brendan-nyhan.com/blog. Using the code from the lab section as a starting point, write a web crawler that starts at the root URL of the blog and collects information about all of its pages. If the blog that you are crawling is too big, then come up with some reasonable constraint, for example, only pages created in the past 2 years.

Your crawler should create a results file that stores the following information about each page in CSV format (BONUS: sort this file chronologically):

- `is_post`: a Boolean value indicating whether your crawler thinks that the page is a post
- `publish_date`: time the article was created
- `author`: author name if available
- `url`
- `post_title`: title of the post
- `comment_count`: number of comments for the post (this may be difficult)

The blog that you are crawling may have a sitemap, but do NOT use it for this exercise. While we will ignore the `robots.txt` file for this exercise only, make sure you abide by the other good citizenship rules (e.g., insert a small delay between requests).

A few other questions to think about as you get started:

- If two pages link to each other, how can you resolve this cycle?
- What are features of the HTML that indicate that this is a post?
- How can you limit your crawl to only the domain of interest?

Reference

1. Durden, T. (2012). *From Chicago to New York and back in 8.5 milliseconds*. https://www.zerohedge.com/news/chicago-new-york-and-back-85-milliseconds. Cited 24 Mar 2018.

Chapter 7
Application Programming Interfaces

Note *In this chapter we demonstrate the use of several publicly available services, including Twitter and Google Maps. If you wish to complete the exercises and examples in this chapter on your own, you may wish to apply for a developer account on each of these services now so that you have it available when you are ready. One reason to do this is that Twitter accounts must go through an approval process than can take several days, and you may wish to have it done before beginning the homework for this chapter.*

In this chapter we will build on your recent experiences working with HTML to discuss Application Programming Interfaces (APIs). As we mentioned before, the web is all about message passing. An API can be thought of as a contract for passing messages: the API designer tells you what inputs they expect, and what data they will give you in return.

Despite their conceptual simplicity, APIs are a very powerful idea that let you build tools to process data from a number of interesting sources. One infamous event in the history of APIs is Jeff Bezos' "Big Mandate" to Amazon employees in 2002[1]:

1. All teams will henceforth expose their data and functionality through service interfaces.
2. Teams must communicate with each other through these interfaces.

Electronic Supplementary Material The online version of this chapter (https://doi.org/10.1007/978-3-030-36826-5_7) contains supplementary material, which is available to authorized users.

---

[1] The source of this is a rant by Google employee Steve Yegge that was accidentally posted publicly on social media [2]. We have heard of the mandate from other sources but could not obtain a copy of the original email.

3. There will be no other form of interprocess communication allowed: no direct linking, no direct reads of another team's data store, no shared-memory model, no back-doors whatsoever. The only communication allowed is via service interface calls over the network.
4. It does not matter what technology they use. HTTP, Corba, Pubsub, custom protocols—does not matter. Bezos does not care.
5. All service interfaces, without exception, must be designed from the ground up to be externalizable. That is to say, the team must plan and design to be able to expose the interface to developers in the outside world. No exceptions.
6. Anyone who does not do this will be fired.

The first two points describe exactly what APIs do, even without using the term: communicate data and functionality. The third point indicates that APIs can serve as an exclusive communication infrastructure for a large company, in part because they are secure. As the fourth and fifth points indicate, APIs serve data on their own terms—the terms of the contract. They provide developers some freedom by abstracting away the underlying implementation details. And of course the final point indicates just how serious Bezos was about this proposal.

In the intervening years Amazon has been able to turn many of their internal tools (e.g., Mechanical Turk,[2] S3,[3] and EC2[4]) into products. This would have been impossible without APIs. The rapid growth of AWS helps to demonstrate the utility of APIs. Now let us take a closer look at how they work and how they can help with research.

7.1 Application Programming Interfaces (APIs)

You already knew about APIs before reading this chapter, even if you did not realize it. If we relax the formal definition for a moment and just think of APIs as contracts for message passing, you have already done this when implementing functions. For example, in Python the code:

```
def foo(bar):
    print(bar)
```

has a contract to accept the argument bar and print its representation.

Building on this, what should a good API do besides take input and return output? First, it should let the customer know when an error has occurred (and, ideally, how to fix it). Second, an API should only throw *documented* exceptions. Third, APIs should be self-documenting, meaning that variable and method names are clear and human-readable.

---

[2] https://www.mturk.com/mturk/welcome.
[3] http://aws.amazon.com/s3/.
[4] http://aws.amazon.com/ec2/.

7.2 REST Is Good

Even within these guidelines there are different ways to have your API send its data over the web. One is "Simple Object Access Protocol" (SOAP), and it is bad. SOAP messages tend to send way too much data. A better option is representational state transfer (REST). Roy Fielding, one of the principal authors of the HTTP spec, first described REST in his dissertation [1].

In a REST API, all things are objects. We do not mean this in quite the same sense as OOP, but it means that we are doing things to other things. If this makes perfect sense to you, do not worry about the alternative. All of the things that the API works with (users, pages, coordinates) have unique URI's, which saves a lot of confusion. All things also have a representation: you already know about the HTML representation, but you could also get the XML or the JSON representation. The important point is that we can elicit different representations of the same object from the API. These features are what make REST APIs so popular.

7.3 More on HTML and HTTP

Since the APIs we will be interacting with use HTTP to send data, we should review a bit more about this protocol and the kind of data we encounter on the web. There were some details about HTML that we intentionally left out of the last chapter. One such minor note is that HTML has a bunch of encoded versions of characters, such as   ("non-breaking space"). Every program that interacts with the web will have a library for dealing with HTML entities. Anything that starts with "&" and ends with ";" is an HTML entity.

Another problem that you may have run into is *relative* URLs. With relative URLs, you do not actually have to specify the root of a page to access it. For example, if we are at www.mattdickenson.com/index.html and want to link to an image, we can specify this as www.mattdickenson.com/assets/python.png or just asssets/python.png. Because developers are lazy (and want to avoid having to update the links of the domain name changes), they will often take the second route. HTML allows us to do this by assuming we want the same root that we are on currently. The Python library urlparse can deal with this through the command urljoin.

See how we handle relative URLs in the following example:

urlparsing.py:

```
1  from urllib.parse import urlparse, urljoin
2
3  url1 = urljoin("http://www.duke.edu", "bob/test.html")
4  url2 = urljoin("http://www.duke.edu", "/")
5  url3 = urljoin("http://www.duke.edu",
            "http://www.google.com")
```

```
 6 url4 = urljoin("http://www.duke.edu",
       "http://www.google.com/test.html")
 7
 8 for url in [url1, url2, url3, url4]:
 9     p = urlparse(url)
10     print("{0}://{1}{2}: {3}".format(p.scheme,
       p.hostname, p.path,
11                                      "is duke" if
       (p.hostname == "www.duke.edu") else "is not duke"))
```

Now that you know a bit more about the way messages are passed over the web, you can better understand the HTTP lifecycle. For much of its life, an HTTP server sits and listens. Then a browser (or some other web node) sends the server a message. These requests typically have one of four types: GET, POST, PUT, and DELETE. GET is used for retrieving objects, such as a blog comment. Objects are created with POST messages. If you want to update an object you use a PUT message. DELETE, as you might guess, is used to delete objects. For example, if you sign up with a new web service,

- a POST message creates your account
- a PUT message updates your email address
- a GET message lets you log in or browse other users
- a DELETE message allows you to destroy your account

When the server receives the message from your browser, it responds as it has been instructed. Normally the server will respect the MIME type you send it, and if it is a REST API it will happily give you back data in HTML, XML, or JSON formats as you prefer. If there was an error in processing the request, you will receive an error code. HTTP has several well-defined error codes in common usage. Here are a few (Table 7.1).

You have probably encountered some of these errors before when browsing the web. If you have seen the Twitter "fail whale," that was a 503 error. In fact, the Twitter API documentation has helpful descriptions of a number of other errors.[5] If you try to send too many requests to the API in a single hour, you will be rate limited and receive a 420 error—this means "enhance your calm".[6]

Table 7.1 HTTP response codes

HTTP code	What it means	What probably happened
200	OK	Something good
404	Not found	Page deleted
500	Internal error	Something is broken
503	Servers busy	Too many requests right now

---

[5] https://developer.twitter.com/en/docs/basics/response-codes.
[6] https://developer.twitter.com/en/docs/basics/rate-limiting.

Notice that both clients (e.g., browsers, `urllib2`) and servers (which host the websites and APIs) use HTTP. There are other protocols for sending data over the web, such as `git://` and `https://`, but you do not need to worry about those for now.

7.4 CRUD

There is another acronym corresponding to REST that you will encounter when discussing what an object can do. CRUD stands for "Create, Read, Update, Delete." When you access this object through HTML, we are using its *read* attribute. POST actions correspond to create, and GET actions correspond to read.

On Twitter, when you read a tweet, you are getting it. When you post it you are creating it. When you delete it, you are deleting it (makes sense, right?). All of these things happen to the same URI, and someone has packaged them into a nice neat library for you.

A URI is made up of 5 things: a domain (or "authority," since it can also include a port), a protocol, a path, a query string, and a hash. You should already be familiar with the domain, protocol, and path. Query strings start with "?" and are concatenated with "&". As you could probably guess, hashes start with "#".

7.5 The Twitter API

We have been using the Twitter API as an example throughout this chapter, but how do you actually use it?

First, you have to register an application with Twitter via https://developer.twitter.com/. You can register even before writing code for your app, although you might want to have a name in mind. Twitter will then give you the access keys you need, which keeps other people from using your app, enables the permissioning system, and keeps track of your rate limiting. You should keep this private.

Next, you will need to install the library `tweepy` with the command `pip install tweepy` in your shell (not the Python console).[7] Twitter will have given you a Consumer Key and a Consumer Secret. Tweepy will need those.

---

[7] If you encounter a problem installing `tweepy` that mentions `"Cannot uninstall 'six'"`, the way around this is to run the command `pip install --ignore-installed six`. Unfortunately, `six` is a notoriously inconvenient library when it comes to introducing conflicts between versions.

The steps you need to follow in order to obtain the required key and secret are:

1. Register for a developer account on https://developer.twitter.com/.
2. Create an "App" in the Twitter Developer web console https://developer.twitter.com/en/apps.
3. Visit the "Keys and Tokens" tab for your app (https://developer.twitter.com/en/apps/YOUR_APP_ID_HERE).

Third, create an API object, which will keep you from having to do all of the things we talked about above as far as getting, posting, etc. See https://developer.twitter.com/en/docs/api-reference-index for all of the cool things you can do with your API. Whenever you interact with APIs, read the documentation before you begin.

This has been a brief introduction, because you will learn it best by actually playing with APIs in the following example, lab session, and homework.

twitter.py:

```
1  #Register an app: https://dev.twitter.com/
2
3  import tweepy
4
5  #First parameter is Consumer Key, second is Consumer Secret
6  auth = tweepy.OAuthHandler('your consumer key', 'your consumer secret')
7  auth.set_access_token('your access token', 'your token secret')
8  api = tweepy.API(auth)
9
10 #See rate limit
11 api.rate_limit_status()
12
13 #Get all tweets in your timeline
14 #    https://dev.twitter.com/rest/reference/get/statuses/home_ti
15 home_tweets = api.home_timeline()
16 for t in home_tweets:
17     #Note: this handles UTF encoded strings by converting them to ASCII format
18     print("{0}: {1}".format(t.user.screen_name.encode('ascii', 'ignore'),
19                             t.text.encode('ascii', 'ignore')))
20
21 #Get a known user
```

```
22 brendan_nyhan = api.get_user('BrendanNyhan')
23
24 #How many favorites does he have?
25 print(brendan_nyhan.favourites_count)
26
27 #Who does Brendan follow?
28 brendans_friends =
        api.friends_ids(id=brendan_nyhan.screen_name)
29
30 for f in brendans_friends:
31     # Note that these are user IDs, not screen names
32     print(f)
```

7.6 Lab Session

This lab will give you experience working with two very useful APIs from the Huffington Post and Google.

7.6.1 Huffington Post

As a first example, we are going to use the Huffington Post Pollster API.[8] Conveniently for our purposes, there is a Python library that makes working with the API simple.[9] Other publishers also offer APIs including *The Washington Post* and *The New York Times*.[10] You can find a whole list of politics-related APIs here: http://www.programmableweb.com/apitag/politics.

7.1 First, everyone needs to install the Python library (`pip install pollster==2.0.2` in your shell). Then, go through the following examples and attempt the challenge at the end.

  `poll.py`:
```
1 import datetime
2 import pollster
3
4 api = pollster.Api()
5
```

---

[8] http://elections.huffingtonpost.com/pollster/api.
[9] http://pypi.python.org/pypi/Pollster.
[10] See https://newsapi.org/the-washington-post-api and https://developer.nytimes.com/.

```
6  # Get a recent chart related to President Trump's job
       approval
7  approval = api.charts_slug_get('trump-job-approval')
8  print(approval.pollster_estimate_summary)
9
10 # Get poll questions related to the 2016 U.S.
       Presidential election
11 questions = api.questions_get(
12     tags='2016-president', # tag of interest
       (commas-separated string)
13     election_date=datetime.date(2016, 11, 8) # date of
       the election
14 )
15
16 # Find the question we want
17 slug_questions = dict([(question.slug, question) for
       question in questions.items])
18 print(slug_questions.keys())
19
20 election_question = slug_questions['16-US-Pres-GE
       TrumpvClinton']
21
22 chart_name = election_question.charts[0]
23
24 # Look up a chart
25 chart = api.charts_slug_get(chart_name)
26
27 print(chart.pollster_estimates)
28 print(chart.pollster_estimate_summary)
29
30 # Limit to Trump vs Clinton questions
31 subset_keys = [k for k in slug_questions.keys() if
       'TrumpvClinton' in k]
32 states = [k.split('-')[1] for k in subset_keys]
33
34 # TODO: in which state was Clinton estimated to be
       leading the most?
35 # TODO: in which state was Trump estimated to be
       leading the most?
```

7.6.2 Google

For the second example, we will use the Google Maps API. As with Twitter, you will need to create a Google developer account at http://developers.google.com. Follow the steps to get an API key listed at https://cloud.google.com/maps-platform/#get-started.[11] You will also have to install the corresponding Python library (`$ pip install googlemaps==3.0.2`).

7.2 Then, work through the following to illustrate getting latitude and longitude from an address, getting address from geocoordinates, using local search, and finding directions. Then, combine all of these tools to iterate through a list of embassy geocoordinates and answer a few questions.

gmaps.py:

```
1  from datetime import datetime
2
3  import googlemaps
4
5  gmaps = googlemaps.Client(key='Your API key here')
6
7  # Geocoding an address to latitude & longitude
8  geocode_result = gmaps.geocode('1600 Pennsylvania
       Avenue, Washington, DC')
9  location = geocode_result[0]['geometry']['location']
10 print(location)
11
12 # Reverse geocode - latitude & longitude to address
13 reverse_geocode_result =
       gmaps.reverse_geocode((38.897096, -77.036545))
14 print(reverse_geocode_result[0]['formatted_address'])
15
16 # Get directions between two locations
17 library_of_congress = '101 Independence Ave SE,
       Washington, DC 20540'
18 white_house = '1600 Pennsylvania Avenue, Washington,
       DC'
19 # mode can be "driving", "walking", "bicycling" or
       "transit"
```

---

[11] Note that you may be required to provide a credit card to set up your account, even if you never exceed the limits of this API's free tier. We do not speak for Google's billing practices, nor are we liable for what they, as an independent entity, may or may not do. Deciding whether to provide Google with your billing information is up to you. If you choose to register for an API key, we believe that the exercise is valuable and informative.

```python
20 walking_directions =
       gmaps.directions(library_of_congress,
21                                           white_house,
22                                           mode="walking"
23                                           )
24
25 steps = walking_directions[0]['legs'][0]['steps']
26
27 for step in steps:
28     print(step['html_instructions'])
29
30 # Get transit directions between the same points
31 now = datetime.now()
32
33 transit_directions =
       gmaps.directions(library_of_congress,
34                                           white_house,
35                                           mode="transit",
36
       departure_time=now
37                                           )
38
39 transit_steps =
       transit_directions[0]['legs'][0]['steps']
40
41 for step in transit_steps:
42     print(step['html_instructions'])
43
44
45 # Look up locations by latitude & longitude
46 embassies = [[38.917228, -77.0522365],
47              [38.9076502, -77.0370427],
48              [38.916944, -77.048739]]
49
50 # TODO: write code to answer the following questions:
51 # which embassy is closest to the White House in
       meters? how far?
52 # what is its address?
53 # if I wanted to get there from the White House by
       transit, what are the directions?
```

Homework

This homework is designed to introduce you the Twitter API and understand their data structures. Due to the fact that tweets themselves are pretty simple, we will be looking at the social graph.

You are going to do some simple analysis on a small portion of the Twitter graph. First identify a *target* Twitter account that has more than 100 followers and followed but less than 1000 (you can do 1000 but it will just take a lot longer). If your own account meets these criteria, use yourself. If not, you can use our accounts (@josh_cutler or @mcdickenson). Starting with the account that you have chosen you will need to determine the people in this person network who meet the following criteria:

- The most followed user that follows your *target*
- The most followed user that has at most 2 degrees of separation from your *target*
- The most active user that has at most 2 degrees of separation from your *target*. You can define most active however you wish, but present your algorithm for computing this explicitly.
- The most active user that your *target* follows. Use the same definition of active that you define above.

Before you get started think about how you wish to define active. It could mean many things.

It is possible that you will hit your Twitter API rate limit while doing your calculations. Think about how you can store the state of your application and then restart when your rate limit is reset.

References

1. Fielding, R. (2000). *Architectural styles and the design of network-based software architectures.* Doctoral dissertation. University of California, California. https://www.ics.uci.edu/~fielding/pubs/dissertation/fielding_dissertation.pdf. Cited 24 Mar 2018.
2. Rowan, R. (2011). *Stevey's Google platforms rant.* https://plus.google.com/112678702228711889851/posts/eVeouesvaVX. Cited 24 Mar 2018.

Chapter 8
Databases

By now you have encountered several ways to structure and store data. The first was as properties of an object, such as `User.name`, but that type of structure had no persistence—it only stayed in memory as long as your program was running. Then we looked at how to read from and write to the disk, which allowed us to store data in both unstructured (plain text) and semi-structured (.csv) formats. After that, we saw that data on the web is organized according to certain conventions and can be served up as a web page or through an API.

In this chapter we are going to introduce a data storage method that combines some of the best features of each of these other formats: databases. Generally speaking, databases allow our program to access data in real time, store it across sessions, give it a useful structure, and share it as necessary.

8.1 Types of Databases

There are many flavors of databases, each with its own advantages and disadvantages. A few of the more popular formats include:

- MySQL[1]
- PostgreSQL[2]

Electronic Supplementary Material The online version of this chapter (https://doi.org/10.1007/978-3-030-36826-5_8) contains supplementary material, which is available to authorized users.

[1] http://www.mysql.com/.
[2] http://www.postgresql.org/.

- SQL Server[3]
- MongoDB[4]
- CouchDB[5]
- Redis[6]

Notice that the first three of these all have some variant of "SQL" in their name. This stands for Structured Query Language. As the name suggests SQL is a standardized way to write database queries, and many popular database formats are based on this standard.

The latter three options above are often referred to as "NoSQL" solutions. Instead of being relational databases, they are formatted in a number of variations including document stores and key-value stores. You can think of key-value stores as similar to the Python dictionaries you have already been using. We will talk more about these in the next chapter.

Database languages fall into the more general category of domain-specific languages (DSLs). DSLs are created with specific problems and solutions in mind, in contrast to general purpose programming languages like Python. For example, regular expressions make up a domain-specific language for parsing text. You could not create a general purpose application using only regular expressions, but for a particular subset of problems they give us a mechanism to express our intended behavior in a powerful way.

As you might expect, databases are a huge topic. Fortunately you can get up and running very quickly and learn as you go. Most of the actual work that goes on with databases is straightforward and involves a small set of queries. It is possible to encounter extreme edge cases involving joins across large numbers of tables or parsing complicated columns, but we will avoid those in these early examples. The point is for you to get hands-on experience storing, querying, and manipulating databases.

8.2 Why SQL?

All "flavors" of SQL (and some other databases) are known as "relational database management systems," sometimes abbreviated as RBDMS. In an RDBMS data are stored in tabular form, with all rows in a given table sharing certain properties. You can think of a single table in a relational database as being very similar to a spreadsheet: it has rows and columns. Each column has a name and each row has

---

[3]https://www.microsoft.com/en-us/sql-server/default.aspx.
[4]http://www.mongodb.org/.
[5]http://couchdb.apache.org/.
[6]http://redis.io/.

8.2 Why SQL?

an index (typically a unique numeric identifier). We can specify relations between these tables as well.

What advantages do databases have over other tabular formats, such as CSVs? The first advantage is that we can quickly run arbitrary queries on the data. CSV files are not optimized for fast searching. If we want to find a row in a CSV file with particular properties, we might have to loop over *all* the rows in order to find it.

Of course, we could achieve a faster lookup of our CSV data by loading it into a more efficient data structure, such as a dictionary where the keys are the values we are interested in. However, if we are interested in several different keys, we might end up loading the data into memory repeatedly. Furthermore, if we have more data than can fit into memory on our machine, then we cannot load the CSV into memory at all. We would have to read it in chunks, which can be time-consuming due to the limitations of reading from disk that we discussed earlier. Databases allow us to store arbitrary amounts of data and can extend beyond what we can fit into RAM at a single point in time.

CSVs also typically only support a single table. Suppose we have two related datasets about a set of countries. The first includes country-specific variables, such as their GDP, population, and levels of inequality. The second includes dyadic data about relations between the countries, such as their levels of trade and whether military conflict exists between them in a given year. If we wanted to predict dyadic conditions using the country-specific variables, we would have to generate a CSV that repeats the country-specific values for every dyad. If we later found out we made a mistake in one of the values (a country's GDP for a given year, for example), we would have to update *every* row in the CSV that contained the mistake. Using a normalized database would avoid this: we could update a single row of our table of country-specific values without worrying about duplication. This might not seem like much of a difference, but when working with large amounts of data, normalization gives you great leverage.

When we talk about databases, two concepts are important: table *schemas* and individual *rows* of data. The schemas in a database are strict. By this, we mean that the database will only return valid data (e.g. no strings when we want a number—if we set it up that way). Going back to our spreadsheet example, the schema defines what columns each table has, how they are named, and what *type* they have.

Another weakness of tabular file formats such as CSVs is that they do not enforce any consistent types on the data. A CSV column could contain strings, integers, floats, and other types, much like a Python list. This flexibility is useful in some cases, but often we wish to enforce consistent types upon all values in a column. Enforcing types can help to prevent accidental data entry errors, too, such as an unexpected string in a numeric column. Knowing that all values in a particular column are of the same type will help us to avoid having to write lots of `if`/`else` logic in our code.

SQL uses slightly different names for types than Python, but conceptually they are very similar. For example, the `int` type corresponds directly to integer in SQL. Strings in Python (`str`) are called varchar types in SQL, referring to a "variable character" field (meaning that it consists of characters and is of indeterminate length).

In addition to type, you can also define the allowable length, whether or not `null` (known as `None` in Python) is allowed, and whether or not uniqueness is required. If you were building a database of Twitter users, you probably would not allow `null` for an account's username, but you might allow an optional field such as a physical address to be `null`.

Enforcing uniqueness prevents duplicate information. You can make sure that values are used only once, such as if you wanted to store information about members of Congress and make sure that no member's data was repeated. If you have a "somewhat unique" field such as a person's name, you can use *joint* uniqueness to ensure that pairs (or larger sets) of columns are collectively unique. For example, you might enforce that user accounts are jointly unique on name and email address. This would allow two people with the same name to each have their own accounts, and for multiple users to share an email address, but no person could create multiple accounts using the same name and email address in combination.

Be careful about what values you assume are unique: often "uniqueness" only holds true at particular scales of data, and when the data size increases dramatically these assumptions can be violated.[7] For this reason, large systems such as web applications often assign users a unique ID. This could be a number that increments every time a new user joins the system or a large random string (with an infinitesimal probability of two users being assigned the same string), known as a "universally unique identifier" or UUID. Regardless of how you decide to determine the unique identifier, every row in a SQL database must have some way to be uniquely identified.

8.3 Schemas

Database schemas perform a number of useful functions. Most importantly, they describe what valid data looks like. They also specify the types of data included in each column of each table. The schema will also specify how indices are generated and whether they are unique. When data is stored in separate tables (you will see examples of this below), the schema also indicates how the various records are connected ("joins").

The schema also helps us to normalize the data. In our country and dyad example above, we would likely have a `country_id` column in our country table, and in our dyadic table we could refer to the nodes in the dyad by `country1_id` and `country2_id` (or any other reasonable nomenclature).

Normalization helps us to identify which rows relate to each other across tables. Say we have a database with three columns, and a value in one of them changes.

---

[7] Recall the popular "birthday problem" example from statistics. In a group of just 23 people, there is about a 50% chance that two of them share the same birthday.

Table 8.1 Book–author database

book_title	author_id
Bible	1
Fahrenheit 451	2
October Country	2
Cat's Cradle	3
Catch 22	NULL

Table 8.2 Database normalizer

1	God
2	Bradbury
3	Vonnegut
4	Tolkien

Table 8.3 Example of an inner join

Bible	God
F451	Bradbury
OC	Bradbury
CC	Vonnegut

The concept of normalization means that the nominal identifier in our database (say, a name) is also assigned a unique identifier (usually a number), so that if a change is made to the nominal identifier, we can still keep track of what happened. It also allows us to make changes quickly, and is optimized for both time and memory.

Relational databases assume that you are going to normalize the data, so they make it very quick to organize tables. Consider the example in Tables 8.1 and 8.2.

Now say we join them using an *inner join*. That would return in Table 8.3.

There are also left and right *outer joins* that work similarly, but will return `Null` for objects that it cannot match. A left outer join makes sure that there is one row in the result for every record in the first part of your query, and a right outer join does the same for the second part of the query. Most of the time you will want to use inner joins or left outer joins.

8.4 Queries

SQL is a rich language for creating database queries with lots of ways to achieve similar outcomes. You should read the documentation for whichever database format you choose. Depending on the database implementation, formatting your queries in certain ways can lead to dramatic speed improvements.

The three most common SQL queries are `SELECT`, `UPDATE`, and `DELETE`. `SELECT` is used to retrieve records that match certain criteria. For example, if we had a table of users and wanted to get all users who were old enough to vote, we might execute a query such as `SELECT * FROM users WHERE age > 18`.[8]

---
[8] Ignore for the moment that we should be stored birth dates, not current ages, in the database if we wanted truly normalized data.

The SELECT * portion of the query means "return all columns in the table." If we wanted a subset of columns we could specify them, such as SELECT name, email_address FROM users .... The FROM users section of the query indicates which table we are pulling the values from. (It is possible that we could have other tables in our database with columns of the same name, such as if we had an employees table). The WHERE age > 18 clause of the query specifies the limitations on the values to be returned. If you are only interested in the *number* of records that match a certain condition (rather than their actual values), you can run a query of the format SELECT count(*) FROM....

We can combine conditions on different clauses, as well. For numeric types we already saw that we can use inequality (> or <). We could also use equality and get users whose age was *exactly* 18 with WHERE age=18. Similarly for a string type, we could look up the user(s) with an exact email address such as WHERE email_address="user@website.com". Depending on which type of database we are using, it might also support partial string matching; if not, you will have to load your results into a general purpose programming language such as Python and do custom filtering there. You can also find values within a subset, such as WHERE state IN ("TX", "CA").

UPDATE modifies records with new data. If we wanted to add full state names to a table that already contained abbreviations, we might run an update query such as UPDATE users SET state_name="Texas" WHERE state_abb="TX". (Again this is a somewhat artificial example because if our database were fully normalized we would have a state_id column in the users table to join to a separate table for states.)[9] UPDATE users indicates the table whose values we intend to change. The SET state_name clause identifies the column(s) we are going to change, and the value that we are setting them to. The WHERE ... section of the query follows all the same behavior we discussed for SELECT statements.

DELETE removes records from the database. This could be used to clean up accidental values or to clear out old data that is no longer needed. For example, if we wanted to delete all accounts created before the year 2000, we could execute a query such as DELETE FROM users where account_created_year < 2000. Deletes are not easily undo-able, so if you are worried about accidentally deleting too much data you might run a SELECT count(*) ... query first with the same conditions to see if it matches more records than you expected. This is also a good reason to keep frequent backups if you delete records often, but for the amount of data we are working with in this chapter that is probably not necessary.

---

[9] Notice that it is conventional for table names to be plural, since they contain many rows.

8.5 Object Relational Mapping (ORM)

Putting data into a database is useful, but as we saw above we are still limited to working with it in a handful of ways. What if we want to operate on the data in a way that is not supported by SQL syntax? At that point, it is time to load your data into a more general purpose programming language such as Python.

As we saw in earlier chapters, when loading data from disk in a format such as CSV, we had very little information about the structure of the data. At best, we could look at the header column of the file and try to make informed guesses about the types of data we would find there (e.g. an "age" column is probably numeric while a "name" column is probably a string). We mostly worked with the table as a list of rows, where the rows themselves were represented as lists or dictionaries.

Now that we are using a database for storage instead, we get all of the benefits mentioned above. Two of the most important of these are that we know the type of each column, and we know all the columns that each table contains. This allows us to form stronger expectations about the data when we retrieve it.

It also allows us to more easily map the rows to Python objects. Instead of treating a row as a list of attributes, we can turn a row from the `users` table into an instance of a `User` object with known properties and behavior.

The tool that allows us to do this is known as an Object Relational Mapping (ORM). As the name suggests, this technique maps records in our relational database to objects in our general purpose language (in this case, Python). We will use the `sqlalchemy` package to provide classes that make setting up our ORM easier. Install this package as you would any other `pip` package, by running `pip install sqlalchemy` from your terminal.

Write the following example in a Python file (a plain-text file ending in .py, e.g. `player.py`):

```
1  from sqlalchemy.ext.declarative import declarative_base
2  from sqlalchemy import Column, Integer, String,
       ForeignKey
3
4  Base = declarative_base()
5
6
7  class Player(Base):
8      __tablename__ = 'players'
9
10     # Have an ID column because player attributes
       (name, etc) are not unique
11     id = Column(Integer, primary_key=True)
12     name = Column(String)
13     number = Column(Integer)
14
15     team_id = Column(Integer, ForeignKey("teams.id"))
```

```
16
17      def __init__(self, name, number, team=None):
18          self.name = name
19          self.number = number
20          self.team = team
21
22      def __repr__(self):
23          return "<Player('%s', '%s')>" % (self.name,
    self.number)
```

In this example, we use `declarative_base` from the `sqlalchemy` library as our base class. This provides a great deal of built-in functionality, so we only have to define a few attributes of our class, how to initialize it, and how to represent it as a string. On lines 5–6, we define the class name and map it to the corresponding table in our database. Note that by convention the class name is singular (`Player`) while the table name is plural (`players`). That is because instances of our class correspond to a single row, not the whole table.

Next, we map attributes of our `Player` class to columns in the database (lines 9–13). As long as the name of the attribute and the column match this is very straightforward. One special attribute here is the **id** column, which we indicate is the primary key (the unique identifier for each row, allowing quick lookup). We also indicate relationships between tables here, such as that the `team_id` column on the `player` table maps to the **id** column in the `teams` table. (We could have also called the column in the teams table `team_id` for clarity, but it is conventional in ORM models for each table to have an **id** column and other tables to refer to that relationship by the singular form of the table name, with the `_id` suffix.)

We then define two methods for our `Player` class (lines 15–21): `__init__` and `__repr__`. You will recall that the `__init__` method defines what happens at the time that an object is instantiated; in this case we simply set its attributes. The `__repr__` controls the behavior of an instance when it is printed (or otherwise included in a string, such as when writing to a file). In this case, `Player` objects display their name and number.

This example continues in more detail, including an ORM class for `Teams`, below.

8.6 In-Class Example

The SQL variant that we will use in this chapter is SQLite.[10] SQLite has several characteristics that make it useful for the examples in this chapter. It comes built-

---

[10] http://www.sqlite.org/.

8.6 In-Class Example

in with Python, making it easy to get started. We will also be using the `pysqlite` module, and you will need to install that separately (`pip install pysqlite`).

SQLite is commonly used for research and data analysis due to its simplicity. Unlike some other versions of SQL, the database itself is stored on your local disk in a simple format. This means that you can share it with other researchers if needed. You could do this by putting it onto an external drive such as a USB stick, sharing over a cloud system such as Dropbox, or even emailing it as an attachment if your dataset is small enough. SQLite may not work for very large or frequently updated datasets (their online guide suggests a rough cut-off of 100,000 daily visitors for a website) but it will work well for most research applications.

In the code below, we set up two ORM classes, add data to our tables, and query them. Work through each short section, relying on the comments to explain the behavior. Try variations on the commands here too, and if your variation does not work try to understand why. Because SQL is such a common tool, you will be able to find answers to your questions on the Internet.

`sqlex.py`:

```
1  # pip install pysqlite
2  import os
3  import sqlalchemy
4
5  from sqlalchemy.ext.declarative import declarative_base
6  from sqlalchemy import Column, Integer, String,
       ForeignKey, and_, or_
7  from sqlalchemy.orm import relationship, sessionmaker
8
9  # Some info about sqlalchemy
10 print(sqlalchemy.__version__)
11
12 # Connect to the local database, can use :memory: to
       just try it out in memory
13 engine =
       sqlalchemy.create_engine('sqlite:///example.db',
       echo=True)
14
15 Base = declarative_base()
16
17 # Define some schemas
18 class Player(Base):
19     __tablename__ = 'players'
20
21     # Have an ID column because player attributes
       (name, etc) are not unique
22     id = Column(Integer, primary_key=True)
23     name = Column(String)
24     number = Column(Integer)
```

```python
25
26      team_id = Column(Integer, ForeignKey("teams.id"))
27
28      def __init__(self, name, number, team=None):
29          self.name = name
30          self.number = number
31          self.team = team
32
33      def __repr__(self):
34          return "<Player('%s', '%s)>" % (self.name,
    self.number)
35
36
37 class Team(Base):
38      __tablename__ = "teams"
39
40      id = Column(Integer, primary_key=True)
41      name = Column(String)
42      players = relationship("Player", backref="team")
43
44      def __init__(self, name):
45          self.name = name
46
47      def __repr__(self):
48          return "<team('%s')>" % (self.name)
49
50 # First time create tables
51 Base.metadata.create_all(engine)
52
53 # See structure of players table:
54 print(Player.__table__)
55
56 # Create a player
57 mason = Player("Mason Plumlee", 5)
58 str(mason.id)
59
60 # Create a session to actually store things in the db
61 Session = sessionmaker(bind=engine)
62 session = Session()
63
64 session.add(mason)
65
66 # Create some more players
67 session.add_all([
```

8.6 In-Class Example

```
68          Player("Miles Plumlee", 40),
69          Player("Seth Curry", 30),
70          Player("Austin Rivers", 0),
71          Player("The other Plumlee", 100)
72  ])
73
74  #Persist all of this information
75  session.commit()
76  str(mason.id)
77
78  # Some querying
79  #order the results
80  for player in
        session.query(Player).order_by(Player.number):
81      print(player.number, player.name)
82
83  # limit the results with offset, might use this for
        pagination
84  for player in
        session.query(Player).order_by(Player.number)[1:3]:
85      print(player.number, player.name)
86
87  # Some filters
88  for player in session.query(Player). \
89                  filter(Player.name == "Mason Plumlee"). \
90                  order_by(Player.number):
91      print(player.number, player.name)
92
93  for player in session.query(Player). \
94                  filter(Player.name != "Mason Plumlee"). \
95                  order_by(Player.number):
96      print(player.number, player.name)
97
98  for player in session.query(Player). \
99                  filter(or_(Player.name == "Mason
        Plumlee", Player.name == "Miles Plumlee")). \
100                 order_by(Player.number):
101     print(player.number, player.name)
102
103 for player in session.query(Player). \
104                 filter(Player.name.like("%Plumlee%")). \
105                 order_by(Player.number):
106     print(player.number, player.name)
107
```

```
108 for player in session.query(Player). \
109        filter(and_(Player.name.like("%Plumlee%"),
       Player.number > 10)). \
110              order_by(Player.number):
111     print(player.number, player.name)
112
113 # Results are just lists
114 results = session.query(Player). \
115           filter(and_(Player.name.like("%Plumlee%"),
       Player.number > 10)). \
116           order_by(Player.number)
117 results.first()
118
119 # Count is faster than loading all of the objects
120 session.query(Player). \
121           filter(and_(Player.name.like("%Plumlee%"),
       Player.number > 10)). \
122           order_by(Player.number).count()
123
124 # How to work with relations
125 duke = Team('Duke')
126
127 players = session.query(Player).all()
128 mason.team = duke
129 players[1].team = duke
130 print(mason.team.players)
131
132 str(duke.id)
133
134 # Lets load the two things together
135 for player, team in session.query(Player, Team). \
136                     filter(Player.name == "Mason
       Plumlee"). \
137                     filter(Team.name ==
       "Duke").order_by(Player.number):
138     print(player.number, player.name, team.name)
139
140 # equivalently
141 for player in session.query(Player).join(Team). \
142                     filter(Player.name == "Mason
       Plumlee"). \
143                     filter(Team.name ==
       "Duke").order_by(Player.number):
```

```
144      print(player.number, player.name, player.team.name)
145
146 # Now some deletion (see SQLAlchemy Cascades for some
        fun data sanitation)
147 print(players)
148 session.query(Player).filter(Player.number ==
        30).count()
149 seth = session.query(Player).filter(Player.number ==
        30).first()
150 session.delete(seth)
151 session.query(Player).filter(Player.number ==
        30).count()
152 print(players)
153
154 # Updating
155 other_plumlee = players[4]
156 other_plumlee.name = "Marshall Plumlee"
157 print(session.dirty)
158 session.commit()
```

8.7 Lab Session

The goal for this lab session is to make sure everyone understands:

- ForeignKey
- relationship
- .query
- .filter
- .group_by
- .order_by
- .distinct()

In previous labs you have worked with both networks and geospatial data. This lab combines those two. For your data, you have information on towns nested in departments, which are further nested in regions (the data is drawn from a French example). You also have the population of each town, along with the distance between towns on *directed* roads.

The code below takes you through the following steps:

8.1

(a) Create the database.
(b) Create the ORM classes.
(c) Create the tables/
(d) Populate the tables with data.

(e) Run queries to answer questions.

The key things to understand from this lesson are how to query data from tables, and how to join multiple tables to show their relationships.

db.py:

```
1  import sqlalchemy
2
3  from sqlalchemy.ext.declarative import declarative_base
4  from sqlalchemy import Column, Integer, String,
       ForeignKey, or_, func
5  from sqlalchemy.orm import relationship, sessionmaker
6
7  #Connect to the local database
8  engine = sqlalchemy.create_engine('sqlite:///geog.db',
       echo=False)
9
10 Base = declarative_base()
11
12
13 # ORM Classes
14 class Region(Base):
15     __tablename__ = 'regions'
16
17     id = Column(Integer, primary_key=True)
18     name = Column(String)
19     departments = relationship("Department")
20
21     def __init__(self, name):
22         self.name = name
23
24     def __repr__(self):
25         return "<Region('%s')>" % self.id
26
27 class Department(Base):
28     __tablename__ = 'departments'
29
30     id = Column(Integer, primary_key=True)
31     deptname = Column(String)
32     region_id = Column(Integer,
       ForeignKey('regions.id'))
33     towns = relationship("Town")
34
35     def __init__(self, deptname):
36         self.deptname = deptname
37
```

```
38      def __repr__(self):
39          return "<Department('%s')>" % self.id
40
41  class Town(Base):
42      __tablename__ = 'towns'
43
44      id = Column(Integer, primary_key=True)
45      name = Column(String)
46      population = Column(Integer)
47      dept_id = Column(Integer,
        ForeignKey('departments.id'))
48
49      def __init__(self, name, population):
50          self.name = name
51          self.population = population
52
53      def __repr__(self):
54          return "<Town('%s')>" % (self.name)
55
56  class Distance(Base):
57      __tablename__ = 'distances'
58
59      id = Column(Integer, primary_key=True)
60      towndepart = Column(String,
        ForeignKey('towns.name'))
61      townarrive = Column(String,
        ForeignKey('towns.name'))
62      # could also use id's
63      distance = Column(Integer)
64
65      td = relationship("Town", primaryjoin=(towndepart
        == Town.name))
66      ta = relationship("Town", primaryjoin=(townarrive
        == Town.name))
67
68      def __init__(self, distance):
69          self.distance = distance
70
71      def __repr__(self):
72          return "<Distance('%s', '%s', '%s')>" %
        (self.towndepart, self.townarrive, self.distance)
73
74
75
```

```python
76  #First time create tables
77  Base.metadata.create_all(engine)
78
79  #Create a session to actually store things in the db
80  Session = sessionmaker(bind=engine)
81  session = Session()
82
83  # Create regions
84  reg1 = Region('Region 1')
85  reg2 = Region('Region 2')
86  reg3 = Region('Region 3')
87  session.add_all([reg1, reg2, reg3])
88
89  # Create departments, nested in regions
90  dept1 = Department('Department 1')
91  reg1.departments.append(dept1)
92
93  dept2 = Department('Department 2')
94  reg1.departments.append(dept2)
95
96  dept3 = Department('Department 3')
97  reg3.departments.append(dept3)
98
99  dept4 = Department('Department 4')
100 reg2.departments.append(dept4)
101
102 session.add_all([dept1, dept2, dept3, dept4])
103
104 # Create towns, nested in departments
105 a = Town('A', 110000)
106 dept1.towns.append(a)
107
108 b = Town('B', 80000)
109 dept3.towns.append(b)
110
111 c = Town('C', 300000)
112 dept3.towns.append(c)
113
114 d = Town('D', 50000)
115 dept2.towns.append(d)
116
117 e = Town('E', 113000)
118 dept2.towns.append(e)
119
```

8.7 Lab Session

```
120 f = Town('F', 70000)
121 dept1.towns.append(f)
122
123 session.add_all([a, b, c, d, e, f])
124
125 ae = Distance(50)
126 ae.td, ae.ta = a, e
127
128 af = Distance(60)
129 af.td, af.ta = a, f
130
131 bc = Distance(50)
132 bc.td, bc.ta = b, c
133
134 bd = Distance(60)
135 bd.td, bd.ta = b, d
136
137 cb = Distance(50)
138 cb.td, cb.ta = c, b
139
140 db = Distance(60)
141 db.td, db.ta = d, b
142
143 de = Distance(30)
144 de.td, de.ta = d, e
145
146 ea = Distance(50)
147 ea.td, ea.ta = e, a
148
149 eb = Distance(60)
150 eb.td, eb.ta = e, b
151
152 ed = Distance(30)
153 ed.td, ed.ta = e, d
154
155 ef = Distance(100)
156 ef.td, ef.ta = e, f
157
158 fa = Distance(60)
159 fa.td, fa.ta = f, a
160
161 session.add_all([ae, af, bc, bd, cb, db, de, ea, eb,
        ed, ef, fa])
162
```

```
163 session.commit()
164
165 # Some example querying
166 for town in session.query(Town).order_by(Town.id):
167     print(town.name, town.population)
168
169 # TODO:
170 # 1. Display, by department, the cities having more
       than 100000 inhabitants.
171 # 2. Display the list of all the one-way connections
       between two cities
172 #    for which the population of one of the 2 cities
       is lower than 80000 inhabitants.
173 # 3. Display the number of inhabitants per department
       (bonus: do it per region as well).
174 # hint: use func.sum
```

Homework

This homework is designed to get you started using databases to store your data.

In this homework you are going to refactor your previous two assignments such that they store information into a database. Specifically:

- **HW5** should store all of the info that you previously outputted to a table called "scrapes." You should add an additional column with a reference to a *Source* model that has the name and URL of the source that you crawled.
- **HW6** should store the Twitter network that you crawled into a local DB, i.e. the user information in a *Users* model. You should have a separate table with a relation to Users that is called "crawls" which specifies a unique crawl and is associated with the attempt to crawl the network (as this information changes over time and we want snapshots). You should at a minimum store the starting user_id for you crawl and the time you initiated it.

Spend some time before you start to sketch out what the schema of your tables will look like. As you refactor, think about how you might have written your code originally to more easily facilitate swapping out the data storage layer.

One nice thing about schemas is that they are a specification for how the data should look (similar to an API). So long as your code conforms to the schema then all of your homework assignments could theoretically be storing their data in some shared data repository.

Chapter 9
NoSQL Databases

The last chapter described how to create, organize, and query information in SQL databases. We started with SQL because it is a very common standard, and even databases that do not share its relational properties often implement a very similar query interface (e.g., CQL for Cassandra). However, sometimes we would like to make different trade-offs than the ones that relational databases have chosen.

There are many popular databases that do not rely on the SQL standard, and they fall into several different types. One type of NoSQL database is a document store (e.g., MongoDB, CouchDB). This means that instead of rows in a table, the individual unit that is stored is a document (more about what this means below). Another NoSQL structure is a graph store (e.g., Neo4j, FlockDB, IBM DB2), which would be useful for the type of data we had in the last lab session and is commonly used by social network services. A third type is key-value storage (e.g., Redis, Riak), which you can think of as a large, persistent dictionary. A final type is NoSQL databases explicitly for text corpuses (e.g., Elastic Search, Solr, Lucene). These help facilitate natural language processing (NLP) based queries.

The NoSQL we will be working with in this chapter is MongoDB, which uses a document store framework.[1] MongoDB is one of the most popular NoSQL database formats. Because it has good support in Python libraries and has clear analogs to the SQL concepts we covered in the last chapter, it is a good choice to illustrate this paradigm.

Electronic Supplementary Material The online version of this chapter (https://doi.org/10.1007/978-3-030-36826-5_9) contains supplementary material, which is available to authorized users.

---

[1] http://www.mongodb.org/.

9.1 Why NoSQL?

If SQL is so popular, why would we ever want to use a NoSQL solution? To answer this, we must first examine what makes SQL and other relational database management systems (RDBMS) popular. One key reason is that RDBMS's use the CAP Theorem. This stands for Consistency, Availability, and Partition tolerance. Consistency refers to the fact that all nodes see the same data at the same time, so if you and I are both accessing a remote database from our local machines we do not have to worry about being on separate versions. Availability is a guarantee that every request receives a response about whether it failed or was successful—you want to be able to get stuff in and out. Partition tolerance means that the system continues to operate even if some elements fail. As you can see, each of these is valuable but also limits what we can do.

A second reason for the popularity of RDBMS are the ACID properties: Atomicity, Consistency, Isolation, and Durability. Atomicity means that each transaction stands on its own, and the whole transaction fails or succeeds (i.e., there are no partial transactions; if any part fails, the database is unchanged). Consistency in this case is slightly different from above, ensuring that any transaction that succeeds maintains the validity of the database. In other words, any successful transaction follows the rules of the database. Isolation ensures that it does not matter whether we execute our transactions serially or concurrently, the result is the same. Finally, durability requires that any transaction that has completed will remain so even if the database goes offline (due to an error, crash, loss of power, and so on). Again, each of these features is desirable in many contexts, but they have the effect of slowing down our transactions with the database.

NoSQL designs sacrifice some of these traits for greater speed and scalability of the database. Ignoring the CAP theorem speeds up operations quite a bit. What do we lose by going with NoSQL? As researchers we are already accustomed to dealing with potential measurement error in our records. A little more noise typically will not hurt you, as long as it is not systematic. If we were implementing a payments system or dealing with medical records these choices might be undesirable, but for the volume and type of information handled in most social science analyses these trade-offs do not come with major downsides.

9.2 How Does NoSQL Work?

MongoDB uses different terminology than SQLite, but many of the concepts are analogous, as you can see in Table 9.1.

You can think of an individual document as equivalent to a Python dictionary. Notice that one concept not included in this table is the idea of a schema: like a dictionary, these documents can include any field that we want. Furthermore, two documents in the same collection will not necessarily contain the same fields. This

Table 9.1 Common concepts in database systems

SQLite	MongoDB
Row	Document
Column	Field
Table	Collection

means that we cannot make as many assumptions about which fields a record will contain, but in return we gain a great deal of flexibility. This flexibility can be useful at the beginning of a project when it is unclear which fields we will eventually need to support. It can also be an advantage when combining data from many different sources for an analysis.

One advantage that MySQL offered was the speedup gained when we indexed records. As long as our query used an index (such as the id of a record), we could retrieve it in $O(\log n)$ time rather than the $O(n)$ time that would be required to loop over all the records in a CSV.

The good news is that MongoDB also supports indices, and an index can be defined on any field of a document. By default all documents in a collection will be assigned a unique `_id` field that will serve as the index. If you index another field, you can choose whether the sort order should be ascending or descending, since MongoDB can traverse the collection in either direction. If you are dealing with time series data, for example, it would be natural to set an ascending index on a `date` or `year` field.

9.3 In-Class Example

To work with MongoDB, you need a MongoDB cluster. For simplicity, we recommend using a free cloud version provided by MongoDB Atlas.[2] Follow the instructions at https://docs.mongodb.com/manual/tutorial/atlas-free-tier-setup/ to set up an account. This takes about 10 min and is completely free for the amount of storage we need for the examples in this chapter.

At the end of the setup instructions, you will get a connection string that looks something like mongodb+srv://<username>:<password>@<host>/test?retryWrites=true&w=majority. We will use this to connect to your database. As with API tokens in previous chapters, keep your password safe and do not commit it with Git.

The next thing you will need is the `pymongo` library and one of its dependencies, `dnspython`:

```
$ pip install pymongo dnspython
```

---

[2]https://cloud.mongodb.com/.

Next we need to create a connection to our MongoDB server, connect to the database we want, and create a collection (analogous to a table in the previous chapter).

mongo.py:

```
 1  # Import required libraries
 2  import datetime
 3  import random
 4
 5  from pymongo import MongoClient
 6  from pymongo import ASCENDING, DESCENDING
 7
 8  # Connection info here - keep this private
 9  connection_string =
        'mongodb+srv://<user>:<password>@<host>/test?retry
        Writes=true&w=majority'
10
11  # Create a client for connecting to the mLab MongoDB
        server
12  client = MongoClient(connection_string)
13  db = client.test
14
15
16  # Next we need to grab our 'collection'
17  # In mongoDB a collection is a bundle of documents.
        Think of it like a table from last week.
18  collection = db.first_collection
```

This code snippet performs several steps as described in the comments. First, we import the libraries we will need. Then, we assign a few variables to hold the connection information. You will need to set the values of `hostname`, `port`, `db_name`, `username`, and `password` yourself. We recommend not committing these values in your Git history, especially if your GitHub repository is public. Then, we instantiate a `MongoClient` object to hold our connection info and authenticate it with the server. Once we have connected to the database, we create a collection called `first_collection`. You can call your collection anything you would like, and as long as you assign it to the variable named `collection` the code below will work without any changes.

After connecting to our collection, we can insert some fake data:

```
29  # Lets make some fake data
30  for i in range(0, 100):
31      collection.insert_one({"author": "Josh",
32                             "text": "Some stuff!",
33                             "tags": ["mongodb", "python",
        "pymongo"],
```

9.3 In-Class Example

```
34                        "date":
     datetime.datetime.utcnow(),
35                        "my_random": random.random() })
36
37 # We can also pass in an array of items all at once:
38 items = []
39 for i in range(0, 100):
40     items.append({"author": "Matt",
41                   "text": "Some other stuff!",
42                   "tags": ["mongodb", "python",
     "pymongo"],
43                   "date": datetime.datetime.utcnow(),
44                   "my_random": random.random() })
45
46 collection.insert_many(items)
```

Here we are inserting 200 documents into the collection. Notice that before inserting the documents we never specified a schema, and there is no reason that any two documents in the collection are required to share the same field names. However, our work will be much easier if we know which fields will be set on the documents and what format they take.

After we create a collection we can run `collection.count()` to see what happened:

```
48 # Lets see what happened
49 db.collection_names()
50 collection.count()
```

If everything worked as expected, you should see a count of 200 documents in the collection.

Once we have added our records, we can retrieve them in various ways:

```
52 # Lets retrieve these documents
53 a = collection.find_one()
54 a['author']       # 'Josh' or 'Matt'
55 a['my_random']    # A random number
56
57 collection.find_one({'author': 'Josh'})
58 collection.find_one({'author': 'Matt'})
```

In the first example we use `find_one()` to retrieve a single record with no filtering. In the second example, we filter on the `author` field. This is analogous to `SELECT * FROM collection WHERE author='Matt'` in SQL. Here are a few other examples of how to translate SQL queries:

We can also chain operations together, such as selecting all records that meet a criteria and counting them:

SQL	MongoDB
SELECT * FROM users	db.users.find()
SELECT * FROM users WHERE age > 18	db.users.find({age: {$gt: 25}})
UPDATE users SET state='Texas' WHERE state='TX'!	db.users.update({state: { $eq: 'TX' } }, { $set: { state: 'Texas' } }, { multi:true })

```
60  # Now lets get multiple results
61  for item in collection.find({'author': 'Josh'}):
62      print(item)
63
64  # You can count with queries as well
65  collection.find({'author': 'Josh'}).count()
```

There are lots of fun operators we can use (see the documentation at http://docs.mongodb.org/manual/reference/operators/). Here is an example with the less-than operator ($lt):

```
69  collection.find_one({'my_random': {'$lt': 0.5}})
70
71  for item in collection.find({'my_random': {'$lt':
        0.5}}).sort('my_random'):
72      print(item)
```

You can also delete all records matching certain criteria:

```
75  collection.remove({'author': 'Matt'})
76  collection.count()
```

Updating a record is similarly straightforward:

```
79  first = collection.find_one()
80  collection.update_one({'_id': first['_id']}, {'$set':
        {'tags': ['a', 'b']}})
81
82  collection.update_many({'my_random': {'$lt': 0.1}},
        {'$set': {'my_random': 0}})
83  collection.find({'my_random': 0}).count()
```

Another useful thing we can do is .explain() where you get Mongo to tell you about how it plans to execute a query. The explain object also has some details such as ['nscanned'] to tell you how many objects it looked at.

Where should we put our index to make querying this data faster? The only thing that differs about our data in this case are the my_random and author fields, so we will use those. Generally you will probably have one or a few fields that stick out as the natural choice for indexing your data, and if not then you can fall back on the _id field that is supplied for you.

```
86 collection.find({"my_random": {"$gt":
      .5}}).sort('author').explain()
87 collection.create_index([("my_random", DESCENDING),
      ("author", ASCENDING)])
```

Notice a few things about these database interactions. First, we never defined a schema. We just used dictionaries of data. Second, no ORM classes were necessary. Any type of data could have gone into any record, anywhere. There is much more you can do with MongoDB, including geospatial indexing and MapReduce operations.[3] You will get some practice with the former in the lab session.

9.4 Lab Session

At the beginning of the lab, discuss the following and make sure everyone is comfortable each concept:

- connecting to a Mongo database
- querying a database
- looping through results
- reading a CSV file in Python
- `Counter()`
- `time.sleep()`

Next, take a look at `campaign.csv`.[4] These are records of every candidate's campaign stops in the 2008 presidential election season. The data was collected from a Washington Post page that is no longer active, using a web scraper similar to the ones you built in an earlier lab session. An automatic geocoding script was then created, using the GoogleMaps API. The geocoded data can be found in `latlong.csv`. This is the data we will be working with.

Use your mLab connection info to connect to your database as in the following example:

9.1 The first thing you will want to do is create your database and populate it with the data from the csv file:

create_db.py:
```
1 import csv
2 import time
3
```

---

[3] http://api.mongodb.org/python/current/examples/geo.html.
[4] Recall that all data associated with the present edition of this text can be found at https://dataverse.harvard.edu/dataverse/python-book.

```python
4  from datetime import datetime
5  from pymongo import MongoClient, GEO2D, ASCENDING
6
7
8  # Connection info here - keep this private
9  connection_string = 'mongodb+srv://<username>:' + \
10     '<password>@<host>/test?retryWrites=true&w=majority'
11
12 # Create a client for connecting to the mLab MongoDB
       server
13 client = MongoClient(connection_string)
14 db = client.test
15
16 # Create a database called 'events'
17 events = db.events
18
19 # input data from csv
20 infile = open('latlong.csv', "r")
21 reader = csv.reader(infile)
22
23 for row in reader:
24     if row[0] != "Date":
25         print(row)
26         date = row[0]
27         # formatted_date = time.strptime(date,
       "%m/%d/%Y")
28         tstruct = time.strptime(date, "%d-%b-%y")
29         formatted_date =
       datetime.fromtimestamp(time.mktime(tstruct))
30         person = row[1]
31         event_type = row[3]
32         city = row[4]
33         state = row[5]
34         lat = float(row[6])
35         lng = float(row[7])
36         events.insert_one({"date": formatted_date,
37                            "candidate": person,
38                            "event_type": event_type,
39                            "city": city,
40                            "state": state,
41                            "latlng": [lat, lng]
42                           })
43 events.create_index([("latlng", GEO2D), ("candidate",
       ASCENDING)])
```

9.4 Lab Session

9.2 Once you have populated your database, try answering the following questions programmatically, using the first query as an example:

nosql.py:

```
1  from collections import Counter
2  from pymongo import MongoClient
3
4  # Connection info here - keep this private
5  connection_string = 'mongodb+srv://<username>:' + \
6      '<password>@<host>/test?retryWrites=true&w=majority'
7
8  # Create a client for connecting to the mLab MongoDB server
9  client = MongoClient(connection_string)
10 db = client.test
11
12 # Assign the 'events' collection to a variable
13 events = db.events
14
15 # queries
16 events.count() # 610
17
18 # 1. Query by candidate: who had most events? who had least?
19 candidates = []
20 for c in events.find({'candidate': {'$gt': "A"}}):
21     candidates.append(c['candidate'])
22 candidate_event_count = Counter(candidates)
23 print(candidate_event_count)
24
25 # 2. Query by state: which had most? which had least?
26
27 # 3. Query by city: which had most events?
28
29 # 4. What was the most frequently occurring event type
       in the most popular city?
30
31 # 5. What other cities are $within the box bounded by
       [40.8, -96.7] and [43.6, -91.6]?
32 # how many events there?
33 # what was the most frequent type of event?
34
```

```
35 # 6. what other cities are within a 100 mile radius
       around 2nd most popular city?
36 # hint: the earth's radius is about 3963.192 miles
37 # how many events there?
38
39 # 7. how many kilometers did the candidate with least
       events travel?
40 # (assume only stops on this itinerary)
41 # what was the avg distance travelled per day?
```

Homework

There is no homework associated with this chapter.

If you are using this material as part of a formal course, we recommend beginning on your final project this week. An example homework that could be assigned is a 1–2 page proposal for the final project, in which students describe what they intend to accomplish and its relevance to the material presented thus far.

If you are studying this material on your own or in an informal setting, one way to check your understanding of the material in this chapter is to find an existing social science dataset, insert it into a MongoDB collection, and run some queries on the data.

Part II
Advanced Topics

The following chapters constitute the "advanced topics" section this book. Each of the remaining chapters is independent, so they need not be covered in sequence. If you are covering this material in a course, you can pick a subset of these chapters that makes sense for the participants in the course.

Chapter 10
Introduction to Machine Learning with Python

Earlier in this book, we mentioned that one reason to learn Python is its popularity in the scientific computing and machine learning communities. This chapter introduces machine learning by demonstrating how to build a classifier from first principles. The lab section then introduces a set of popular libraries for data analysis.

In the first few chapters of this book, the code you wrote used **if** branches to change its behavior based on properties of the data at hand. Then, in the previous two chapters we showed how to extend this logic to database queries. In each case, however, the thresholds used for comparisons were determined by us as developers. This chapter will show how to use a more data-driven approach with machine learning.

Machine learning refers to a branch of computing in which the intended behavior for a program is *learned* from data rather than being explicitly programmed by a human. One way to categorize machine learning problems is whether they are *supervised* or *unsupervised*. If an approach is supervised, that means that the ML algorithm is taught using training data that includes example inputs and outputs. Linear regression (OLS) is a common example of a supervised learning problem. Unsupervised approaches attempt to learn structure in data without explicit training labels. Clustering (e.g., k-means) is an example of unsupervised learning.

Supervised learning problems are further subdivided into *classification* and *regression* approaches. Classification problems are those with discrete (nominal) output. For example, determining whether an image contains a picture of a human face or not is a classification problem. Regression problems, on the other hand, have

---

Electronic Supplementary Material The online version of this chapter (https://doi.org/10.1007/978-3-030-36826-5_10) contains supplementary material, which is available to authorized users.

continuous output.[1] Predicting the GDP of a country based on the characteristics of its political and legal systems is an example of a regression problem.

In this chapter we will describe how to build one of the easiest to understand and most mathematically tractable classifiers, known as a naive Bayes classifier. This type of classifier is straightforward to implement and tends to work well on a wide variety of problems. The structure of the classifier is such that it takes some set of input features and produces a list of probabilities that the input belongs to each of k output classes.

We will use the following terminology to describe this classification approach:

- what you want to classify (the *document*)
- *features* of the document
- which *features* you want to emphasize for classification (i.e., which will be good predictors)
- the *categories* you wish to sort your documents into (aka "labels")

Suppose, for example, that we have a set of email documents and want to classify them as spam or not spam. The documents would be the set of emails. The features of each email would include the body text, sender address, and other metadata such as the time at which the message was sent. Of these features, we would select a few that we expect will help us to discriminate between the two output classes. The label in this case is binary (spam/not spam).

10.1 Bayes' Rule: Review and Example

Our classifier makes use of Bayes' Rule, so it will be helpful to take a moment to review how it works. Bayes' Rule is about taking some known conditional probability and using it to calculate other unknown conditional probabilities. For the email example, we could write out the probability that a document is spam, given the observed features, via Bayes' Rule as:

$$P(\text{spam} \mid \text{features}) = \frac{P(\text{features} \mid \text{spam}) P(\text{spam})}{P(\text{features})}$$

We will use what is called the "bag of words" approach. In the example above, our features are word counts. The "bag of words" approach only deals with individual words rather than phrases. This means that we throw away some of the structure of the document since we are not considering the sequential nature of the words. We choose this because evaluating all of the n-grams in a large text

---

[1] When dealing with a large output domain, many problems with discrete answers can be well-approximated by regression approaches. For example, if we aim to predict the population of a state, it would not make sense to predict fractional values, but there are so many potential output values that classification approaches are untenable.

10.2 Metrics: Precision and Recall

Spam	Not spam
Offer is secret	Play sports today
Click secret link	Went play sports
Secret sports link	Secret sports event
	Sports is toddy
	Sports cost money

document quickly becomes intractable. To deal with this, we look at the text with the assumption that words appear independently. Note that this is a huge assumption that does not hold in reality, but it makes the problem much simpler and works well in many practical applications.

Suppose that our training set consists of the eight labeled documents below, and that our only feature is the body of each message.

Here is an example from the Stanford AI course:

Let us use this data to estimate the conditional probabilities:

$$P(\text{``secret''} \mid \text{spam}) = \frac{3}{9} = \frac{1}{3}$$

$$P(\text{``secret''} \mid \text{notspam}) = \frac{1}{15}$$

$$P(\text{spam} \mid \text{``sports''}) = \frac{P(\text{``sports''} \mid \text{spam})P(\text{spam})}{P(\text{``sports''} \mid \text{spam})P(\text{spam}) + P(\text{``sports''} \mid \text{not spam})P(\text{not spam})}$$

$$= \frac{\frac{1}{9} \times \frac{3}{8}}{\frac{1}{9} \times \frac{3}{8} + \frac{1}{3} \times \frac{5}{8}}$$

$$= \frac{\frac{1}{24}}{\frac{6}{24}}$$

$$= \frac{1}{6}$$

We can compute this probability for each word in our corpus, and then consider the probability of spam/not spam given the entire contents of the document. Notice that one disadvantage of this approach is that we will not know how to deal with any words that do not appear in our training data, so we will have to ignore them. In practice we would like to have a much larger training set than in the illustration above.

10.2 Metrics: Precision and Recall

In the example above, notice that our classes are *imbalanced*: there are fewer messages in the training set that are spam than not spam. This type of imbalance is very common in political and social datasets. For example, only a small fraction of country-pair dyads are at war in any given year because war is an infrequent occurrence. There are many approaches for handling this imbalance that are beyond the scope of this chapter.

For now, it is sufficient to observe that we may not want to use 50% as our threshold just because this is a binary output problem. The actual threshold that we choose depends on our preferences over Type I versus Type II errors. This preference might cause us not to make 50% our threshold for categorization. Two quantities that are commonly used to evaluate binary classifiers are *precision* and *recall*.

Continuing with the spam classification example, let us refer to any spam message that is accurately predicted to be spam as a "true positive" (tp) and any non-spam message that is classified as not spam as a "true negative" (tn). Spam messages that are incorrectly labeled as not spam are "false negatives" (fn), while non-spam that is accidentally labeled as spam are "false positives" (fp). When deciding on which thresholds to use, we must consider the trade-off between the latter two categories: how bad is it to let a spam message get into a user's inbox, versus incorrectly labeling a valid message as spam? Precision and recall let us evaluate these trade-offs.

Precision, p, is defined as

$$p = \frac{|tp|}{|tp| + |fp|}$$

Lower precision, then, means a higher rate of false positives.

Recall, r, is similarly defined as

$$r = \frac{|tp|}{|tp| + |fn|}$$

Lower recall, then, means a higher rate of false negatives. Notice that one property of these metrics is that they ignore the number of true negatives since they are considered irrelevant for many applications.

Ideally, we would like a classifier with perfect precision and recall rates ($p = r = 1.0$), but in practice achieving higher rates of precision means lower rates of recall and vice versa. Choosing different thresholds for your binary classifier will result in different points along the precision/recall curve, so you must choose how much to weight each type of error.

10.3 LaPlacean Smoothing

A problem with Bayes' Rule is that, as we noted above, in the naivest of cases is that it does not know how to handle inputs it has not seen before. One approach to handle this is LaPlacean smoothing. Smoothing in this case refers to adding a small constant and re-adjusts according to the rules of probability to ensure that we never assign a message a 0% probability of being spam.

Compare the naive (ML) and Laplace-smoothed (LS) estimators below:

$$\text{ML} p(x) = \frac{\text{count}(x)}{N}$$

$$\text{LS} p(x) = \frac{\text{count}(x) + k}{N + k|x|}$$

Notice that the LS estimate converges to the ML estimator when the number of categories $|x|$ is large. In any case k is a small, arbitrary constant. You can choose k to make your in- and out-of-sample accuracy as high as possible. $k = 1$ is usually a good place to start.

10.4 Implementing a Classifier

A minimal-working example of this type of classifier consists of three things:

1. a dictionary with words as keys and probabilities as values
2. a method to train the classifier
3. a prediction method to run the classifier on new data

Recall from our discussion of data structures why a dictionary makes the most sense for mapping words to probabilities: we do not know a priori which words we will encounter, and we want fast lookup when we do encounter a word. Knowing a bit about data structures makes this task much easier than if we had used, say, a linked list.

Some other terms to keep in mind when implementing are:

- word breaking: a method to seperate groups of characters into their constituent words.
- word stemming: a method to recognize that "angry" and "anger" each consist of "angr-" and are thus functionally equivalent for purposes of classification (often this results in a substantial improvement in probability calculation)
- stop words: words like "in, at" and "the" can lead to spurious results and take up space in your data storage, so most folks ignore them

For a more in-depth discussion of some of these concepts see Chap. 14

There are libraries that help with all of these operations in Python, which is part of what makes it nice to work with for this type of problem. (Note that all of our examples today are English-specific; word stemming may not work in many languages, and word breaking can be extremely hard.)

In our classifier, we may also want to differentiate words depending on what feature they came from. For example, "Viagra" in the subject line of an email is more likely to indicate spam than if it appears in the body of an email.

We will need the ability to *train* our classifier based on existing data. This is where we use word breaking, word stemming, and stop words in the process of generating features from our training data.

Once we have trained our classifier we are ready to take it out in the real world and do some classification. Note that in addition to your training data you should also have a set of test data that you hold out. Using your test data to check out-of-sample accuracy can prevent you from over-fitting your classifier to the training data.

Below is an example of a naive Bayes classifier that breaks the text into features and categorizes names by gender. Depending on the actual problem we might care more about Type I or Type II errors. Notice also that when everything is scaled by the same denominator, the denominator becomes irrelevant. Many classification algorithms get a small speed and memory advantage from disregarding the denominator completely.

naivebayes.py:

```
1  # Some docs for this library:
2  # http://www.nltk.org/api/nltk.classify.html
       #module-nltk.classify.naivebayes
3  # pip install nltk
4
5  import random
6  import nltk
7  nltk.download('names')
8
9  from nltk.corpus import movie_reviews, names
10
11 names = ([(name, 'male') for name in
       names.words('male.txt')] +
12         [(name, 'female') for name in
       names.words('female.txt')])
```

This code loads the Python Natural Language Toolkit (nltk), which includes a corpus of male and female names. We load these names, with their labels, and shuffle them. The order in which we present the names to our classifier does not matter, but shuffling allows us to easily subset them into training and testing sets as shown below:

```
15
16 # Our simple feature
17 def gender_features(word):
18     return {'last_letter': word[-1]}
19
20 featuresets = [(gender_features(n), g) for (n, g) in
       names]
```

10.4 Implementing a Classifier

Notice that here our only feature is the last letter of the word. We would not expect this to be a very accurate classifier, but it serves to illustrate the process of deriving features from raw data.

```
21 train_set, test_set = featuresets[500:],
       featuresets[:500]
22 classifier = nltk.NaiveBayesClassifier.train(train_set)
23
24 classifier.classify(gender_features('Neo'))
25 classifier.classify(gender_features('Trinity'))
26 classifier.classify(gender_features('Max'))
27 classifier.classify(gender_features('Lucy'))
28
29 # Check the overall accuracy
30 print(nltk.classify.accuracy(classifier, test_set))
31
32 # Lets see what is driving this
```

Here we initialize the classifier, train it on our training set, and explore a few examples. As you would probably expect this is not a very accurate classifier at first but it gives us a baseline to improve upon.

```
35
36 # Lets be smarter
37 def gender_features2(name):
38     features = {}
39     features["firstletter"] = name[0].lower()
40     features["lastletter"] = name[-1].lower()
41     for letter in 'abcdefghijklmnopqrstuvwxyz':
42         features["count(%s)" % letter] =
   name.lower().count(letter)
43         features["has(%s)" % letter] = (letter in
   name.lower())
44     return features
45
46 featuresets = [(gender_features2(n), g) for (n, g) in
     names]
47 train_set, test_set = featuresets[500:],
     featuresets[:500]
48 classifier = nltk.NaiveBayesClassifier.train(train_set)
```

Here we do the same as above but with additional features: the first letter of the name, counts of how often each letter appears, and a binary value of whether each letter appears in a name or not. Notice that other than the first and last letter, these features ignore the structure of the name. This means that a typically male name such as "Ernie" has almost identical features to the typically female name "Irene."

When two inputs have very similar features but different output classes, this makes it quite difficult for our classifier.

What can we do in this case? One option is to increase the size of our training set:

```
50
51  # Still not great.... How can we refine?
52  train_names = names[1500:]
53  devtest_names = names[500:1500]
54  test_names = names[:500]
55  train_set = [(gender_features2(n), g) for (n, g) in
        train_names]
56  devtest_set = [(gender_features2(n), g) for (n, g) in
        devtest_names]
57  test_set = [(gender_features2(n), g) for (n, g) in
        test_names]
58  classifier = nltk.NaiveBayesClassifier.train(train_set)
```

Inspecting the names for which we made the wrong classification could also help us to understand why the classifier is making mistakes:

```
60
61  # Lets look at the errors and see if we can do better
62  errors = []
63  for (name, tag) in devtest_names:
64      guess = classifier.classify(gender_features2(name))
65      if guess != tag:
66          errors.append((tag, guess, name))
67
68  for (tag, guess, name) in sorted(errors):
69      print('correct=%-8s guess=%-8s name=%-30s' % (tag,
        guess, name))
70
71  # yn seems to be female even though n seems to be
        male.  ch tends to be male even though h is female
72  def gender_features3(word):
73      return {'suffix1': word[-1:],
74              'suffix2': word[-2:]}
75  train_set = [(gender_features3(n), g) for (n, g) in
        train_names]
76  devtest_set = [(gender_features3(n), g) for (n, g) in
        devtest_names]
77  classifier = nltk.NaiveBayesClassifier.train(train_set)
```

Another, larger dataset in the nltk package is a set of movie reviews. Since these are multi-word documents, this will allow us to look at an example that is closer to the spam classification problem that motivated this chapter.

```
# Now lets look at some bigger documents
nltk.download('movie_reviews')
documents = [(list(movie_reviews.words(fileid)),
    category)
            for category in movie_reviews.categories()
            for fileid in
    movie_reviews.fileids(category)]
random.shuffle(documents)

all_words = nltk.FreqDist(w.lower() for w in
    movie_reviews.words())
keys = all_words.keys()
word_features = list(keys)[:2000]

def document_features(document):
    document_words = set(document)
    features = {}
    for word in word_features:
        features['contains(%s)' % word] = (word in
    document_words)
    return features

print(document_features(movie_reviews.words
    ('pos/cv957_8737.txt')))

featuresets = [(document_features(d), c) for (d, c) in
    documents]
train_set, test_set = featuresets[100:], \
    featuresets[:100]
classifier = nltk.NaiveBayesClassifier.train(train_set)

print(nltk.classify.accuracy(classifier, test_set))

classifier.show_most_informative_features(5)
```

The simple bag-of-words approach does not result in a very accurate classifier, but it helps to demonstrate a very simple starting point for natural language processing (NLP). We cover NLP in more detail in Chap. 14.

10.5 Lab Session

In this chapter we will look at other data analysis tools available in Python. In particular we will focus on the pandas library.

Getting started with `pandas` can be a bit tricky because it relies on the `NumPy` and `SciPy` libraries, which are notoriously difficult to install. Anaconda has made this process much easier. The specific requirements we need to run the code in this lab are:

- `numpy` (should already have this)
- `pandas` (for data handling)
- `statsmodels` (for modeling)
- `matplotlib` (for plotting)

If you used a recent version of Anaconda to install and manage your Python environment, these packages should already be included and set up. However, if you have any trouble setting up these packages, we suggest making use of http://www.pythonanywhere.com. It is free to log in and run a console, and already has `pandas`, `numpy`, and `scipy` installed. Python Anywhere can also be useful for doing collaborative coding with a classmate or fellow researcher.

If you wish to run this code on your local machine without Anaconda, you will need to install `pandas`, `numpy`, `scipy`, and `statsmodels`. You can do this with `pip`. If you run into trouble, we recommend searching for the "SciPy superpack" and following those instructions.

10.1 Using the data supplied in `states.csv` file in our dataverse,[2] work through the following exercises to see how to load and inspect data in pandas. Note that the CSV file must either be in the same directory as your Python file/session or you must specify a fully qualified path (you can get the full path by right-clicking and choosing "Get Info" on MacOS). By the end of it you will be fitting your own linear model.

10.5.1 Series

`data.py`:

```
1  from pandas import Series
2  import pandas as pd
3  import numpy as np
4  import statsmodels.api as sm
5
6  # create a data series - basically an array
7  my_series = Series([4, 3, 5, np.nan, 6, 8])
8  print(my_series)
9  print(my_series.values)
10 print(my_series.index)
```

---

[2]https://dataverse.harvard.edu/dataverse/python-book.

10.5 Lab Session

Here we are using a data structure class, `Series`, supplied by the pandas library. Series work very much like lists. One key difference is that instead of being indexed from 0 to n, we can supply a custom index:

```
12 my_series2 = Series([3, 5, 7, 9], index=['d', 'c',
       'a', 'b'])
13 print(my_series2)
14 print(my_series2.values)
15 print(my_series2.index)
```

Another benefit o f`Series` is that we can use logical indexing on them, such as selecting the subset of values that exceed a given threshold. We can also perform operations on all values of a Series directly, without using list comprehensions:

```
17 # Series work kind of like lists
18 print(my_series[1])
19 print(my_series2['d'])
20 print(my_series2[['c', 'a', 'd']])
21 print(my_series2[my_series2 > 0]) # equivalent to
       which() in R
22 myDoubled = my_series * 2 # perform functions
23 print(np.exp(myDoubled))
```

The index of a series behaves much like the keys in a dictionary:

```
25 # Series indices can be thought of like dicts, but are
       immutable
26 print('b' in my_series2)
27 print('e' in my_series2)
```

In fact, the similarity between dictionaries and series is so strong that we can easily initialize a Series using a dictionary:

```
29 # We can even turn dicts into series
30 eVotes = {'NC': 15, 'TX': 38, 'CA': 55} # sorted by key
31 ev = Series(eVotes)
32 states = ['CA', 'NC', 'TX', 'OH']
33 ev2 = Series(ev, states)
```

`Series` and their indices also have a name attribute that we can set if we are dealing with several `Series` in the same program:

```
35 # Series have a name, as do their indices
36 ev2.name = "electoral votes"
37 ev2.index.name = "state"
38 print(ev2)
```

10.5.2 DataFrames

`Series` are one-dimensional data structures. Given their similarity to lists and dictionaries, their value may not be very apparent at first. However, when we extend this to the two-dimensional `DataFrame` the value should be more clear. `DataFrames` are tabular structures, similar to a spreadsheet or database table. We can initialize dataframes directly from a CSV file. The file can be local or a URL on the web:

```
43 data = pd.read_csv("states.csv")
44 print(data.head())
45 print(data['State'])
46 # change column names for convenience
47 data.columns = ['st', 'yr', 'ev', 'pop']
```

In addition to the columns read in from the CSV, we can also derive new columns:

```
49 # we can create new columns
50 data['popm'] = data['pop'] / 1000000.0
51 data['evs'] = data['ev'] -3
52 data.head()
53 del data['evs']
54 data.head()
```

The `head()` function allows us to see the first five rows of the dataframe, similar to the `head` command in Unix shells.

Like `Series`, dataframes also have indices:

```
56 # DataFrames can be indexed
57 print(data[1:4])
58 print(data[data['yr'] == 2010])
59 print(data[data['ev'] > 40])
```

We can also apply functions to columns:

```
66 fmt = lambda x: '%.2f' % x
67 data['popm'].map(fmt)
```

If we want to sort on a particular column (similar to ORDER BY in a SQL query), we can do that too:

```
70 data2 = data.sort_index(by='popm')
71 data2.head()
72 data2.tail()
```

Like `head()`, `tail()` shows the *last* five rows in the dataframe.

If we want to compute a variety of summary statistics on the dataframe, we can that with the following commands:

10.7 Plotting

```
1 data.shape
2 data.mean()
3 data.median()
4 data.std()
5 data.sum()
```

For convenience, there is also a single command that will compute many of the same summary statistics in addition to the 25th, 50th, and 75th percentiles of the values: `data.describe()`.

Using these commands, to answer the following questions:

1. How much did total population change between 1990 and 2010?
2. How many people did the average member of Congress represent in 1990?

10.6 Linear Modeling

The pandas model also easily supports linear regression using ordinary least squares (OLS):

```
94 model = sm.OLS(data['ev'], data['popm']).fit()
95 print(model)
96 print(model.params)
```

This code computes a simple univariate regression model, with population as the input and the number of electoral votes as the output. The `model.beta` attribute gives us the coefficients of the model.

10.7 Plotting

In addition to using summary statistics, plotting data is also useful for exploratory analyses. To do this, we will use the `matplotlib` library. Although its charts are not the most visually appealing, this is one of the simplest plotting libraries in Python.

```
1 import matplotlib as plt
2
3 fig = plt.figure()
4 plt.xlabel('Population')
5 plt.ylabel('Electoral Votes')
6 plt.title('Roundabouts and Safety')
7 plt.scatter(data['popm'], data['ev'])
8 plt.show()
9 fig.savefig("graph1.png")
```

The `plt.figure()` line initializes a figure that we can add attributes to. The `xlabel` and `ylabel` commands set the labels for the *x* (horizontal) and *y* (vertical) axes, respectively. `title` controls the text that appears above the figure. The `scatter` command products a bivariate scatterplot. `plt.show()` displays the figure, and `savefig` saves it to a file.

We can also add the line of best fit from our regression model by creating a column to store the predicted values:

```
 1 data['yhat'] = model.beta['intercept'] +
     model.beta['x'] * data['popm']
 2
 3 fig = plt.figure()
 4 plt.xlabel('Population')
 5 plt.ylabel('Electoral Votes')
 6 plt.title('Roundabouts and Safety')
 7 plt.scatter(data['popm'], data['ev'])
 8 plt.plot(data['popm'], data['yhat'], 'r')
 9 plt.show()
10 fig.savefig("graph2.png")
```

The main difference here is the line `plt.plot(data['popm'], data['yhat'], 'r')`, which adds the line of best fit in red (`'r'`).

10.8 Further Reading

Pandas is a very powerful library, and it can also handle a variety of computations that we have not covered here such as what to do with missing values and computing first-differences for time series.

If you are interested in learning more about data analysis with Pandas and Python, we recommend the following resources:

- *Python for Data Analysis* by Wes McKinney
- http://blog.yhat.com/posts/logistic-regression-and-python.html
- http://blog.yhat.com/posts/setting-up-scientific-python.html
- http://pandas.pydata.org/getpandas.html
- http://ipython.org/ipython-doc/dev/interactive/htmlnotebook.html

Chapter 11
Linear Programming

In this chapter we present another facet of the world of computational social science. One very useful but under-utilized toolkit is linear programming.[1] The name does not refer to computer programming, but to programming in the sense of "planning." It was developed in the context of military planning, and traces its roots to the simplex algorithm [2].

Linear programming (LP) is an advanced topic from a computer science perspective, because the way that it works is technically difficult. Rather than present the technical underpinnings, we will discuss LP from a data modeling perspective.

Think of linear programming as a way to solve an optimization problem. By framing the optimization as a linear program, it can be solved efficiently using algorithms like Dantzig's and others. That is, we seek a solution to *minimize*, *maximize*, or *equality*, subject to some constraints. If you have solved a set of linear equations for a variable, you have done this. If you have ever worked on game theory or economics, you have dealt with maximization (and possibly minimization). In calculus you can also sometimes format problems as linear problems. For computers, these problems are easily solvable.

Electronic Supplementary Material The online version of this chapter (https://doi.org/10.1007/978-3-030-36826-5_11) contains supplementary material, which is available to authorized users.

[1] By social scientists, that is for an exception in the recent political science literature, see [1].

11.1 PuLP

The Python package we will use in this chapter is PuLP.[2] Under the hood, PuLP relies on the GNU Linear Programming Kit (GLPK), which you will also need to have installed on our system for these programs to work.[3] For installation instructions, see https://www.gnu.org/software/glpk/#downloading for MacOS and Linux or https://sourceforge.net/projects/winglpk/files/latest/download for Windows. After downloading and opening one of the archives such as `glpk-4.15.tar.gz`, read the `INSTALL` text file for further instructions. MacOS users also have the option to use Homebrew for installation, using the command `brew install glpk` (we recommend this approach if you are familiar with Homebrew). In addition, you will need to `$ pip install pulp` regardless of which operating system you use.

11.2 Example: Paintings

Linear programming can be difficult to understand in the abstract, so it is better if we focus on a few examples. First, suppose you are consulting for a mediocre artist who can create two different paintings. One of them sells for $30 and the other sells for $20. To make the $30 painting, we need four units of blue paint, one unit of green paint, and one unit of red paint. The painting that sells for $20 requires two units of blue, two of green, and one of red. She has sixteen units of blue, eight of green, and five of red. Given these constraints, how can the artist maximize her revenue?

What makes this amenable to a linear program is all in how we set up the problem. One way to solve this would be to draw two-dimensional indifference curves. However, we can also set up our constraints as a series of equations:

$$\text{maximize: } 3x + 2y$$
$$\text{blue: } 4x + 2y \leq 16$$
$$\text{red: } x + y \leq 5$$
$$\text{green: } x + 2y \leq 8$$

Similarly for the linear program, we indicate what we want to maximize and what the constraints are (Note that we have scaled the prices of the paintings by a factor of ten.)

---

[2] https://pypi.python.org/pypi/PuLP.
[3] https://www.gnu.org/software/glpk/.

11.2 Example: Paintings

painting.py:

```
1  from pulp import *
2
3  # declare your variables
4  x = LpVariable("x", 0, cat=LpInteger)
5  y = LpVariable("y", 0, cat=LpInteger)
6
7  # defines the problem
8  prob = LpProblem("painting", LpMaximize)
9
10 # defines the objective function to maximize
11 prob += 3*x + 2*y
12
13 # defines the constraints
14 prob += 4*x + 2*y <= 17
15 prob += x + 2*y <= 9
16 prob += x + y <= 6
17 prob += x>=0
18 prob += y>=0
19
20 GLPK().solve(prob)
21
22 # Solution
23 for v in prob.variables():
24     print(v.name, "=", v.varValue)
25
26 print("objective=", value(prob.objective))
```

Going through this code step-by-step will help to show how we can instantiate linear programming problems in Python.

First, we import the pulp library. Then we set up our two variables, x and y. We give each one a lower bound of zero, no upper bound, and specify that they must be integer values (LpInteger). We could also specify these as constraints in our problem setup (e.g., x >=0, y >= 0) but doing it at the time that we set up the variables helps to prevent us from making mistakes.

We then set up the problem, specifying that it is a maximization problem. The first part of the problem that we specify is the objective, that is, the function that we are seeking to maximize. Then, we enumerate the constraints. We could set these up in any order. The function that we pass without an greater-than/less-than/equality constraint is treated as the objective, while any others are treated as constraints.

The call to GLPK().solve() then finds the solution, which we print to the console.

As you can see, once you can set up a problem as a set of linear equations, it is trivially easy to solve. The cleverness is all in setting up the problem. The following sections go through additional examples to make this process more concrete.

11.3 Example: Airlines

Now consider another example, a fictional airline industry. Each airline covers a few continents. No single airline covers every continent, so we must find a combination if we wish to cover all six (populated) continents. We are trying to determine the minimum number of airlines to deploy from the set in the table below to get full global coverage.

Airline	Continents covered
A	NA, SA, Af
B	E, Af, As
C	NA, Au, E
D	SA, As, E
E	Af, As, Au
F	NA, E

$$\text{minimize: } A + B + C + D + E + F$$
$$\text{NA: } A + C + F \geq 1$$
$$\text{SA: } A + D \geq 1$$
$$\text{Af: } A + B + E \geq 1$$
$$\text{E: } B + C + D + F \geq 1$$
$$\text{As: } B + D + E \geq 1$$
$$\text{Au: } C + E \geq 1$$

Notice that this set of equations fully specifies the problem we are trying to solve. We can write this as a linear program and see that ABC and DEF are both solutions. Lack of uniqueness is one downside to linear programming, but if all you care about is finding some feasible solution this is sufficient.

airline.py:

```
1  from pulp import *
2
3  prob = LpProblem("airline", LpMinimize)
4
5  # Variables
6  a = LpVariable("airline_a", 0, 1, LpInteger)
7  b = LpVariable("airline_b", 0, 1, LpInteger)
8  c = LpVariable("airline_c", 0, 1, LpInteger)
9  d = LpVariable("airline_d", 0, 1, LpInteger)
10 e = LpVariable("airline_e", 0, 1, LpInteger)
11 f = LpVariable("airline_f", 0, 1, LpInteger)
```

```
12
13  # Objective
14  prob += a + b + c + d + e + f
15
16  # Constraints
17  prob += a + c + f >= 1
18  prob += a + d >= 1
19  prob += a + b + e >= 1
20  prob += b + c + d + f >= 1
21  prob += b + d + e >= 1
22  prob += c + e >= 1
23
24  GLPK().solve(prob)
25
26  # Solution
27  for v in prob.variables():
28      print(v.name, "=", v.varValue)
29
30  print("objective=", value(prob.objective))
```

We follow the same process here that we did above, first initializing the problem with a name and then setting up our variables. By specifying lower bounds of 0, upper bounds of 1, and integer solutions, we constrain each variable to be binary. We then want to *minimize* the total number of airlines involved (a + b + c + d + e + f) while still covering every continent (the constraints). When you run the program you will see that it is possible to cover all six populated continents with only three airlines.

11.4 Set Partitioning

Linear programming can also be used for handling set partitioning problems. Set partitioning problems determine how the items in a set S can be split into smaller subsets. A set *cover* requires all items to be in at least one partition, while a set *packing* requires all items to be in zero or one partition.

To motivate this problem, suppose that we are organizing an event for diplomats from various countries. The diplomats themselves are the elements of S, and they must each be seated at exactly one table (the partitions). As the event coordinator, we wish to maximize the total happiness of each table.

The first thing that we will define is our variables (the maximum number of tables at our event, the maximum number of diplomats at each table, and the total list of diplomats, in this case represented by letters).

```
1 max_tables = 5
2 max_table_size = 4
3 diplomats = 'A B C D E F G I J K L M N O P Q R'.split()
```

Let us assume for the sake of this problem that each diplomat's ideology can be represented in a single dimension. We further assume that the happiness of a particular table is maximized when the maximum ideological distance between its members is minimized. We can now define the happiness function:

```
7 def happiness(table):
8     """
9     Find the happiness of the table
10    """
11    return abs(ord(table[0]) - ord(table[-1]))
```

One way to solve this problem is to list out every possible solution and examine the value of our objective function (in this case, total happiness) for that particular solution. You can see that this would quickly become intractable for large sets but it will work well for small examples and demonstrates the power of linear programming.

```
13 #create list of all possible tables
14 possible_tables = [tuple(c) for c in allcombinations(diplomats,
15                             max_table_size)]
```

For each of these combinations (3213 in total), we can indicate whether they are used or not with a binary variable. As we saw in the airline example, enumerating six binary variables quickly became very repetitive. To avoid writing over 3000 lines of code for this problem, we will instead use the LpVariable.dicts function to set up our variables using the list of possible tables.

```
18 x = LpVariable.dicts('table', possible_tables,
19                     lowBound = 0,
20                     upBound = 1,
21                     cat = LpInteger)
```

Now we are ready to set up our problem (again as a minimization of the total number of tables), the objective function (happiness) and the constraints (maximum number of tables):

```
23 seating_model = LpProblem("Seating", LpMinimize)
24
25 seating_model += sum([happiness(table) * x[table] for table in possible_tables])
26
27 seating_model += sum([x[table] for table in possible_tables]) <= max_tables, \
28                             "max_number_of_tables"
```

Our final set of constraints is that each diplomat must be seated at exactly one table:

```
31  for diplomat in diplomats:
32      seating_model += sum([x[table] for table in
        possible_tables
33                                     if diplomat in table])
        == 1, "must_seat_%s"%diplomat
```

We can then solve the problem and print the solution:

```
35  seating_model.solve()
36
37  print("The chosen tables are out of a total of
        %s:"%len(possible_tables))
38  for table in possible_tables:
39      if x[table].value() == 1.0:
40          print(table)
```

This is another example where multiple optimal solutions exist. This example should give you ideas for many other political science models that can be instantiated as linear programs.

11.5 Feasibility

In all of the examples above, we sought integer solutions. Sometimes finding the integer solution can take a great deal of time or even be infeasible (not possible), but you can still find the frontiers of the feasibility space if you search for a non-integer solution.

Notice that the solution technique here can also be applied to game-theoretic problems, including normal form games. There are many strategies for solving such games, and using the minimax theorem with linear programming is one such solution. If this interests you, see the work of Vincent Conitzer, among others.[4]

References

1. Cutler, J., De Marchi, S., Gallop, M., Hollenbach, F. M., Laver, M., & Orlowski, M. (2016). Cabinet formation and portfolio distribution in European multiparty systems. *British Journal of Political Science, 46*(1), 31–43.
2. Van Dantzig, D. (1947). On the principles of intuitionistic and affirmative mathematics. *Indagationes Mathematicae, 9*, 429–440.

---

[4]http://www.cs.duke.edu/~conitzer/.

Chapter 12
Practical Programming

As you start to write more complex programs and deal with larger data sets, you will encounter more edge cases. Examples of this include missing data, data that is not in the type that you expected, or difficulty converting between various formats required by external APIs. Many of these errors cannot be detected until runtime (in part due to Python's dynamic typing but this is not entirely to blame).

In this chapter, we describe two strategies for addressing such issues. The first is to develop a better understanding of *exceptions* and how to handle them. The second is to write automated tests—code that checks the behavior of other code—to verify the behavior of your programs. These strategies can be used in conjunction to control what your code does when it encounters unexpected circumstances. Since both of these strategies are widely used by working programmers, we refer to these topics collectively as "practical programming."

12.1 Exceptions

By this point there is a good chance that you have already encountered exceptions when running your code. Perhaps you have seen them already and not quite understood what was happening. Any time that Python seemingly "explodes" it is most likely because an unhandled exception has been raised.

What is the difference between an exception and an error? Many programmers use them interchangeably, so usage is somewhat inconsistent. In this text, we use

---

Electronic Supplementary Material The online version of this chapter (https://doi.org/10.1007/978-3-030-36826-5_12) contains supplementary material, which is available to authorized users.

© Springer Nature Switzerland AG 2020
J. Cutler, M. Dickenson, *Computational Frameworks for Political and Social Research with Python*, Textbooks on Political Analysis,
https://doi.org/10.1007/978-3-030-36826-5_12

"exception" to describe a *potential* error. However, if the exception is anticipated and handled correctly by your code, errors can be avoided.

We saw in chapter two that everything in Python is an object, and exceptions are no... exception. Exceptions are a way of passing messages back and forth about something that has gone wrong or an unexpected behavior. Because exceptions are objects, they follow the same class/instance pattern as the example objects we discussed in the previous chapters. Exception is a class, and all types of exceptions inherit from this class. Any exception based on the class Exception will have a message attribute (what prints when the exception is raised) and a way to retrieve the stack trace (which identifies where the error occurred). Note that **raise** is a keyword in Python, referring to when the exception message is sent. Here is how we can define a custom exception:

custom_exception.py:

```
1  # CustomException inherits from Exception
2  class CustomException(Exception):
3      def __init__(self, value):
4          self.value = value
5
6      def __str__(self):
7          return self.value
```

When an exception is raised, one of two things can happen. If the exception is uncaught (the default), it will stop the execution of your program. To prevent the exception from interrupting the program we can "catch" the exception. Caught exceptions are ones that keep the user from doing something the programmer does not want them to do, or to keep running despite a known error. A good rule of thumb with exception handling is if you know what to do with an error, handle it; if not, let it percolate up.

To handle exceptions, we can set up a **try...except** block around the code where we think a problem might happen. This block bears a resemblance to the **if...else** blocks you have seen already. As soon as an exception is thrown in your **try** block, the interpreter does not execute anything else—it jumps immediately to the **except** block. The code below demonstrates exception handling with several exceptions that can occur, building on our CustomException code above. Uncomment lines 18, 19, or 20 (one at a time) to see how the various exceptions are raised and handled. If you are curious about what happens when a code path might result in multiple subsequent errors, you can also uncomment lines 18–20 all at once.

custom_exception.py:

```
1  import traceback
2
3  # CustomException inherits from Exception
4  class CustomException(Exception):
5      def __init__(self, value):
6          self.value = value
```

12.1 Exceptions

```
 7
 8      def __str__(self):
 9          return self.value
10
11  def i_call_a_function_with_errors():
12      try:
13          print("Calling a function....")
14          #function_with_generic_error()
15          #function_with_custom_error()
16          #function_with_unknown_error(1)
17          print("Tada!")
18      # 'as' gives us access to the exception
19      except CustomException as inst:
20          print("Custom Error Caught!
    Error({0})".format(inst.value))
21      except: # any exception is caught, even ones you
    don't know about
22          print("Default Error Caught!")
23      else: # if nothing broke, then run this block
24          print("No error raised.")
25          traceback.print_exc() # this prints the
    traceback
26      finally: # this block is always run
27          print("Goodbye!")
28
29  def function_with_generic_error():
30      # this method doesn't know what to do with the
    exception
31      raise Exception("Foo!")
32
33  def function_with_custom_error():
34      # this will be handled in the function above
35      raise CustomException("Foo Bar!")
36
37  def function_with_unknown_error(foo):
38      foo.bar()
39
40  i_call_a_function_with_errors()
```

So how does the **try** statement work? The execution starts immediately after the **try** statement and continues until an exception occurs. If an exception occurs, the execution stops there and jumps to the **except** clause, where it will be handled if it is the type of exception named after **except** (or a subclass of the type that is named). If the exception is not a handled type, it will percolate up, because it is possible that the exception is handled in an outer scope.

Line 28 might also look unusual to you. Here we are importing the `traceback` module in order to print a stack trace of any errors that occurred. (If no errors occur, this statement will print No error raised.) You are probably accustomed to seeing all **import** statements at the beginning of a file, which is generally the best practice. However, in some cases you only need a particular dependency for certain code paths. For example, if you have a script that runs a statistical analysis but only need to update your visualizations occasionally, you might prefer to import Matplotlib inside a class or function that handles your visualization output. You do not need to worry about the import occurring multiple times—Python caches your dependencies, so once the module is loaded it will not be imported again.

If no exception occurs during the **try** clause, the **except** clause is skipped. For code that you want to only execute if an exception was *not* raised during the **try** block, you can include an **else** clause. If there is behavior that you want to ensure occurs whether an exception is raised or not, you can optionally add a **finally** block.

```
1  def divide(x, y):
2      try:
3          result = x / y
4      except ZeroDivisionError:
5          print("division by zero!")
6      else:
7          print("result is", result)
8      finally:
9          print("executing finally clause")
```

You can see the behavior of the **else** and **finally** clauses in the following examples:

```
>>> divide(42, 14)
result is 3
executing finally
>>> divide(42, 0)
division by zero!
executing finally
>>> divide("42", "2")
executing finally clause
Traceback (most recent call last):
  File "<stdin>", line 1, in <module>
  File "<stdin>", line 3, in divide
TypeError: unsupported operand type(s) for /: 'str'
    and 'str'
```

Notice that the **finally** clause occurs even if an unhandled exception is raised. Why might you want to use a **finally** clause? Typically you will want to use this any time that you need to ensure that the side effects of your code need to be cleaned up—saving output to a file (or closing it, if you are not using a context manager), closing a database connection, or updating your cursor if you are paginating through data.

Exception handling will be useful as you implement more complex programs, and when you are dealing with data from an outside source such as an API. High quality APIs will document the exceptions that various calls can raise so that you know how and when to handle them. If you write code that raises custom exceptions, it is a good idea to document those as well—and to write tests for them, as we discuss in the next section.

12.2 Testing

Software testing is a big topic, and many good books have been written exclusively on this subject. There are many types of software testing. The main distinction is between manual testing (where other developers imitate users and play around trying to break things) and automated testing (where the developers specify desired behavior and use test cases to verify that the program behaves as expected).

We are going to use automated testing—that is, code that we write to test our other code. Within the world of automated testing there is still a great deal of variety. "Unit tests" check whether a small chunk of code behaves as expected. For example, does add(2, 2) function return 4? "Integration tests," on the other hand, check whether different parts of the code play together nicely. An example of this is checking whether the client code for an API works well with the server code.

12.2.1 Motivation for Testing

The basic idea is to use *more* code to test your "real" code and make sure it does what it is supposed to. This probably seems like a lot of work but almost always pays off for projects that are maintained and extended over time. The probability that testing will pay off goes to one asymptotically with the size of the project.

Automated tests are frequently used for a variety of purposes. The first is to verify correctness: does the code do what you expect? When working programmers are assigned tasks to write code for a particular purpose, demonstrating the behavior with passing tests can be one criterion for considering their task complete. Another motivation is to catch regressions, or bugs that are introduced after the initial work on a piece of code is complete. This often happens by accident as a piece of code grows increasingly complex and is worked on by different programmers over time, none of whom may ever have the full context for what the intended behavior is in each code path.

Tests can serve as documentation, helping readers to see what the code is actually supposed to do. If you are collaborating or someone else inherits your code, it helps them to have a test suite to detect which portions of the code are more complex or prone to exceptions. In a sense, testing allows you to be "lazy" since you do not have to hold all the potential code paths in your head at once.

Testing also forces you to write better code. Writing testable code will require you to avoid doing things like calling `random.random()` in the middle of a function, since testing random code is substantially more complicated than testing deterministic code.[1] Writing tests will also help you to better understand the behavior of your code: if you truly understand what code is supposed to do, you should be able to assert what output it should give you

12.2.2 Practicing Unit Tests

Tests are particularly useful for dynamic languages like Python, which has no static type checking. That is because we often have certain expectations of what inputs or outputs will look like (strings versus integers, for example) that are not actually defined in our code. To see what we are talking about, let us review the purpose of unit testing and then actually write some code.

Unit tests are meant to exercise all non-trivial methods in our code. The two things that we check for are *correctness* and *robustness*. Correctness asks, "does the code do what we want it to when we give it the right input?" Robustness asks, "how does the code handle unexpected inputs?" A third aspect we sometimes want to test is performance, but generally this is a separate step from testing since it involves collecting metrics and determining which are acceptable and which are not.

In addition to testing all of the important code ("code coverage"), good tests should be short and succinct. This serves two ends. First, testing small chunks of your code allows you to find where problems are better than checking larger parts. Second, you want your test suite to run quickly so that you will not be hesitant to use it. A good benchmark is that it should take 10 s or less to run your tests, although for larger applications this is not always feasible.

Tests can have three outcomes: pass, fail, or error. In Python's `unittest` library, these are represented with three different symbols: ".", "F", and "E", respectively. When all of your tests pass, this is sometimes known as "green" status (because of the colors that print out in most testing libraries). A failure ("red") means something did not go as expected. An error message means that the code did not execute completely—this can be worse than a failing test.

---

[1] One common approach to this would be to add a `randomizer` argument to your function. In your tests, you can pass a `randomizer` that is in fact deterministic, and thus know exactly what the behavior should be at runtime. This practice is known as "dependency injection" and is frequently a useful strategy for making code more testable.

12.2 Testing

The testing process is iterative:

1. See a bug. ("red")
2. Write a test.
3. Fix the code so that it satisfies the test. ("green")
4. Improve the code so that it is simpler/faster while still passing tests. ("refactor")
5. Repeat.

Again, the argument for using automated testing is that your mind will be more open (and thus write more appropriate tests) before you develop the tunnel vision that comes with writing code in a certain way.

Here is an example of a function that returns the ordinal string representation of a number:

ordinal.py:

```
1  def ord_number(number):
2      # Handle teens
3      if abs(number) > 10 and abs(number) < 20:
4          return str(number) + "th"
5
6      # Get the last digit (with proper negative handling)
7      last_num = abs(number)%10
8
9      # Handle few special cases
10     if last_num == 1:
11         return str(number) + "st"
12     elif last_num == 2:
13         return str(number) + "nd"
14     elif last_num == 3:
15         return str(number) + "rd"
16
17     return str(number) + "th"
```

By convention, if the code we are testing lives in a file called foo.py, our tests go in a file called test_foo.py (often in a directory specifically for tests, since we often run all tests at once). Here are some example tests for our ordinal code:

test_ordinal.py:

```
1  import unittest
2
3  from ordinal import ord_number
4
5  class TestInClassCode(unittest.TestCase):
6
7      def test_one(self):
8          self.assertEqual(ord_number(1), "1st")
```

```
 9
10      def test_two(self):
11          self.assertEqual(ord_number(2), "2nd")
12
13      def test_three(self):
14          self.assertEqual(ord_number(3), "3rd")
15
16      def test_four(self):
17          self.assertEqual(ord_number(4), "4th")
18
19      def test_eleven(self):
20          self.assertEqual(ord_number(11), "11th")
21
22      def test_negative(self):
23          self.assertEqual(ord_number(-3), "-3rd")
24
25 if __name__ == '__main__':
26      unittest.main()
```

If you run `test_ordinal.py`, you should see output like the following, indicating that all tests passed successfully:

```
1 ......
2 ----------------------------------------------------------------------
3 Ran 6 tests in 0.000s
4
5 OK
```

Notice a few things about these tests. First, we do not enumerate *all* inputs. If we know that the behavior of our code is the same for all numbers between 10 and 20 (exclusive), then we only have to use one value from this interval in our test. Second, any time we have a special case—behavior that applies for only one input value, or a small range of input values—we should add a test for that. Deciding which tests to write for your code is more art than science, but these general rules will help you as you get started with automated testing.

12.3 Lab Session

12.3.1 Starter Code

Use the following code as a starting place for this lab. The comments under each function name describe the intended purpose of the function. The current implementation only shows how certain parts of the function might work—it is **not**

12.3 Lab Session

intended to be correct. Your job is to turn this into working code that passes the tests. For more detail on what is expected, see the test suite below.

numeric_functions.py:

```python
 1  def binarify(num):
 2      """convert positive integer to base 2"""
 3      if num <= 0:
 4          return '0'
 5      digits = []
 6      while num:
 7          digits.append(str(num % 2))
 8          num /= 2
 9      digits.reverse()
10      return ''.join(digits)
11
12  def int_to_base(num, base):
13      if num == 0 or base <= 0:
14          return '0'
15      digits = []
16      absnum = abs(num)
17      while absnum:
18          digits.append(str(absnum % base))
19          absnum /= base
20      if num < 0:
21          digits.append('-')
22      digits.reverse()
23      return ''.join(digits)
24
25  def base_to_int(string, base):
26      if string == "0" or base <= 0:
27          return 0
28      elif string[0] == "-":
29          rev = (string[1:])[::-1]
30      else: rev = string[::-1]
31      result = 0
32      for i, num in enumerate(rev):
33          result += int(num) * base ** i
34      if string[0] == "-":
35          result *= -1
36      return result
37
38  def flexibase_add(str1, str2, base1, base2):
39      num1 = base_to_int(str1, base1)
40      num2 = base_to_int(str2, base2)
41      tmp = num1 + num2
```

```
42      result = int_to_base(tmp, base1)
43      return result
44
45  def flexibase_multiply(str1, str2, base1, base2):
46      num1 = base_to_int(str1, base1)
47      num2 = base_to_int(str2, base2)
48      tmp = num1 * num2
49      result = int_to_base(tmp, base1)
50      return result
51
52  def romanify(num):
53      if not 0 < num < 4000:
54          return "out of range"
55      ints = (1000, 900, 500, 400, 100, 90, 50, 40, 10,
        9, 5, 4, 1)
56      nums = ('M', 'CM', 'D', 'CD', 'C', 'XC', 'L',
        'XL', 'X', 'IX', 'V', 'IV', 'I')
57      result = ""
58      for i, base10 in enumerate(ints):
59          count = int(num / base10)
60          result += nums[i] * count
61          num -= base10 * count
62      return result
```

12.3.2 Tests

If the following tests pass, your implementation can be considered correct. However, there may be edge cases that are not covered by these tests. Which ones can you think of?

test_numeric_functions.py:

```
1  import unittest
2
3  from numeric_functions import *
4
5  class TestLab1Code(unittest.TestCase):
6
7      def setUp(self):
8          self.x_base2 = "10000"
9          self.y_base2 = "10"
10         self.y10 = "2"
11         self.xplusy = "10010"
12         self.xtimesy = "100000"
13
14     # Correctness tests
```

12.3 Lab Session

```
15      # binarify
16      def test_binarify_16(self):
17          self.assertEqual(binarify(16), "10000")
18
19      def test_binarify_127(self):
20          self.assertEqual(binarify(127), "1111111")
21
22      def test_binarify_0(self):
23          self.assertEqual(binarify(0), "0")
24
25      def test_binarify_negative(self):
26          self.assertEqual(binarify(-16), "0")
27
28      # int_to_base
29      def test_int_to_base_2(self):
30          self.assertEqual(int_to_base(123, 2),
    binarify(123))
31
32      def test_int_to_base_3(self):
33          self.assertEqual(int_to_base(12, 3), "110")
34
35      def test_int_to_base_10(self):
36          self.assertEqual(int_to_base(16, 10), "16")
37
38      def test_int_to_base_0(self):
39          self.assertEqual(int_to_base(16, 0), "0")
40
41      def test_int_to_base_negative(self):
42          self.assertEqual(int_to_base(-16, 2), "-10000")
43
44      # base_to_int
45      def test_base_to_int_16(self):
46          self.assertEqual(base_to_int("10000", 2), 16)
47
48      def test_base_to_int_3(self):
49          self.assertEqual(base_to_int("110", 3), 12)
50
51      def test_base_to_int_10(self):
52          self.assertEqual(base_to_int("16", 10), 16)
53
54      def test_base_to_int_0(self):
55          self.assertEqual(base_to_int("123", 0), 0)
56
57      def test_base_to_int_negative(self):
```

```
58            self.assertEqual(base_to_int("-10000", 2), -16)
59
60    # flexibase methods
61    def test_flexibase_add_base_2(self):
62        self.assertEqual(flexibase_add(self.x_base2,
      self.y_base2, 2, 2), self.xplusy)
63
64    def test_flexibase_add_base_2_10(self):
65        self.assertEqual(flexibase_add(self.x_base2,
      self.y10, 2, 10), self.xplusy)
66
67    def test_flexibase_multiply_base_2(self):
68
      self.assertEqual(flexibase_multiply(self.x_base2,
      self.y_base2, 2, 2), self.xtimesy)
69
70    def test_flexibase_multiply_base_10(self):
71
      self.assertEqual(flexibase_multiply(self.x_base2,
      self.y10, 2, 10), self.xtimesy)
72
73    # romanify
74    def test_romanify_3(self):
75        self.assertEqual(romanify(3), "III")
76
77    def test_romanify_9(self):
78        self.assertEqual(romanify(9), "IX")
79
80    def test_romanify_10(self):
81        self.assertEqual(romanify(10), "X")
82
83    def test_romanify_49(self):
84        self.assertEqual(romanify(49), "XLIX")
85
86    def test_romanify_99(self):
87        self.assertEqual(romanify(99), "XCIX")
88
89    def test_romanify_3999(self):
90        self.assertEqual(romanify(3999), "MMMCMXCIX")
91
92
93 if __name__ == '__main__':
94     unittest.main()
```

Try writing tests that fail, demonstrating that the code does not support the use case that your test describes. Then, update the starter code so that the *all* the tests—the existing ones and the new ones you added—pass.

Chapter 13
Case Study: Image Processing

This chapter introduces techniques for working with imagery in Python. First, we review the data formats commonly used for storing images. Popular formats such as JPG, PNG, and TIF can all be treated as multidimensional arrays. Converting images to a format that can be used in tabular data analysis requires additional steps to extract features of interest.

Then, we work through a research question using satellite observations of nighttime lights. Is the level of radiance that a city emits at night a useful proxy for predicting population levels? We show how to obtain, process, and analyze satellite imagery to investigate this question. We then provide examples of other political research questions that are amenable to this type of analysis.

The code in this chapter will also leverage several skills that you learned in earlier chapters. You will use data parsing skills for working with JSON and CSV files (see Chap. 6). Acquiring geospatial data for the cities of interest will also require making calls to an external API, Google Maps, as you did in Chap. 7. Our analysis will use NumPy and Pandas, similar to the classification task in Chap. 10. The data visualization tools that you used in that chapter will also be useful for visualizing results.

Throughout this chapter we also illustrate, in case study fashion, how to conduct a reproducible data analysis project in Python. There are three files that constitute the core of the analysis. `fetch_data.py` retrieves publicly available data and provides helper functions for loading it. Then, `preprocessing.py` extracts features of interest. Finally, `analysis.py` fits models and visualizes results. These steps are flexible enough to be adapted to a wide range of applications and provide a basis for creating your own research workflow using Python.

Electronic Supplementary Material The online version of this chapter (https://doi.org/10.1007/978-3-030-36826-5_13) contains supplementary material, which is available to authorized users.

© Springer Nature Switzerland AG 2020
J. Cutler, M. Dickenson, *Computational Frameworks for Political and Social Research with Python*, Textbooks on Political Analysis,
https://doi.org/10.1007/978-3-030-36826-5_13

13.1 Working with Image Data

Why would political and social scientists want to work with imagery? We suggest three key motivations: images are *ubiquitous*, they are *semantically rich*, and (given the skills that you have learned in this text, as well as recent developments in the field of computer vision) this work is *computationally tractable*.

Images contain a great deal of meaning. As the saying goes, "a picture is worth a thousand words." Consider three famous photographs: *V-J Day in Times Square*,[1] showing a returning sailor kissing a woman in a white dress; *Tank Man*,[2] in which an unidentified man faces a column of tanks in Beijing; and *Situation Room*,[3] which shows President Barack Obama with his national security team during the raid that resulted in the death of Osama bin Laden. Each of these images has the power to convey a mood and an experience of a particular time and place that is nearly impossible to communicate with words alone.

Furthermore, images are omnipresent in political contexts. News reports, campaign advertisements, and social media posts all use the power of images to communicate messages.[4] The political impact of images is especially acute in wartime photographs (such as the raising of the U.S. flag at Iwo Jima) and in video (e.g., the conventional wisdom that televised debates contributed to John F. Kennedy's defeat of Richard Nixon in the 1960 U.S. presidential election) [9].

If images are so important, why has their use in political research been heretofore quite limited? One reason is that until the advent of social media, the volume of imagery produced was rather small: there might be only a handful of nationally or internationally significant images published each year. As of 2017, users on a single social network (Instagram) had posted over 40 billion photos. Of course only a small portion of these contain politically relevant messages, but the ability to view photos in near-real time taken at political events such as campaign stops, town hall events, and protests represents historically unparalleled access to visual information. Given the reduced costs for data storage and computation associated with cloud computing, researchers now have the ability to ingest, store, and process these images. Developments in the world of computer vision are also becoming available to non-experts through APIs such as Google Cloud Vision,[5] Amazon Rekognition,[6] and Microsoft Azure.[7]

---

[1] https://en.wikipedia.org/wiki/V-J_Day_in_Times_Square.
[2] https://en.wikipedia.org/wiki/Tank_Man.
[3] https://en.wikipedia.org/wiki/Situation_Room_(photograph).
[4] For an overview of the role of images and video in U.S. presidential campaigns, see [3].
[5] https://cloud.google.com/vision/.
[6] https://aws.amazon.com/rekognition/.
[7] https://azure.microsoft.com/en-us/services/cognitive-services/computer-vision/.

13.1.1 Data Formats

13.1.1.1 JPG, PNG, and TIFF

Working with images requires first understanding how they are stored. Three of the most popular formats used are JPG, PNG, and TIF. These formats share many common properties, but this section briefly describes their differences.

JPG (or JPEG, an abbreviation for Joint Photographic Experts Group, the organization that introduced the format in 1987) is one of the oldest formats still in widespread use. One reason for its popularity is that it allows for the compression of images. Because images tend to contain a great deal of redundant information (e.g., many pixels of blue sky in an outdoor photo), they can often be stored in much less space than would be required for the uncompressed data. However, this compression is *lossy*, meaning that the original image cannot be recovered from the compressed version without some distortion.

One of the main distinctions between PNG (Portable Network Graphics) and JPG images is that the former format uses *lossless* compression. In other words, it takes advantage of the same redundancy that JPG does but allows for better recovery of higher-resolution images. The PNG format also offers better support for a transparency layer than JPG does.

The TIF (Tagged Image File) format was originally developed for use with image scanners in the 1980s. One major difference between TIF and the previous two formats is its ability to contain metadata about the image. In other words, you can think of a TIF file as a container for both an image (which may itself be a JPG or another compressed format) and a description of the image. This description is particularly valuable for aerial and satellite images, because users need a method for mapping between spatial coordinates and pixel coordinates. We show how to use this information from a TIF file later in this chapter.

13.1.1.2 Common Characteristics of Image Data

Regardless of the format used to store the data, certain abstractions apply to all of the image types you are likely to encounter. Digital images contain *pixel values* organized in a *multidimensional array* and possibly organized into multiple *channels*.

The simplest image array to work with is a binary (black and white) image, in which zero represents white pixels and one represents black pixels.[8] One of the most popular datasets for computer vision research, MNIST, consists of 28 × 28 pixel binary images representing handwritten digits. See Fig. 13.1 for an example

---

[8]This is by convention; you could easily reverse the assignment of pixel values to colors and obtain the inverse image.

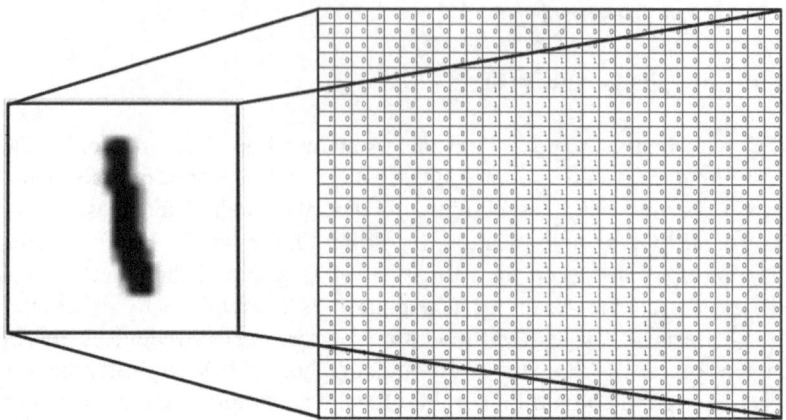

Fig. 13.1 MNIST example

of how the digit "1" could be stored as a two-dimensional binary array. A 32-by-32 binary image would require 1024 bits (128 bytes) of memory.[9]

Of course, most images contain more information than just black-and-white binary values. A greyscale image can also be represented as a two-dimensional array. If we allow one byte (8 bits) per pixel, we can store pixel values as integers between 0 and 255 (2^8 total values). Our hypothetical 32-by-32 image could then be stored using one kilobyte of memory (1024 pixels of one byte each).

To include color information, we introduce multiple *channels*. Instead of a two-dimensional array, we have a 3D array where the third dimension is the channel index. The most common ordering system is RGB: the first channel represents the red intensity of the pixel, the second channel represents green, and the third blue.[10] Using three bytes to represent each color gives us a much larger colorspace than greyscale images: $256^3 = 16,777,216$ possible values for each pixel. Since the number of colors is combinatorial in the number of channels, the color space we can use grows much faster than the memory consumption of our multi-channel images. Using our 32-by-32 image example again, storing pixel values in RGB space would require three kilobytes of memory (Fig. 13.2).

Other channels and color spaces could be used as well. For example, if we allow transparency in our image (as the PNG format does), we could add an "alpha" channel for our transparency layer and use RGBA order. Seeing channels in other orders such as BGR (blue-green-red) is also common, so you should inspect your data if you are not sure about the order. Other common color spaces include HSV (one channel each for the hue, saturation, and value of the color) and CMYK (cyan, magenta, yellow, and black channels). In the following two subsections we show how to work with images in Python, including conversion between color spaces.

---

[9]The actual size on disk when stored in a conventional format would be larger due to the required header information.
[10]https://en.wikipedia.org/wiki/RGB_color_model.

13.1 Working with Image Data

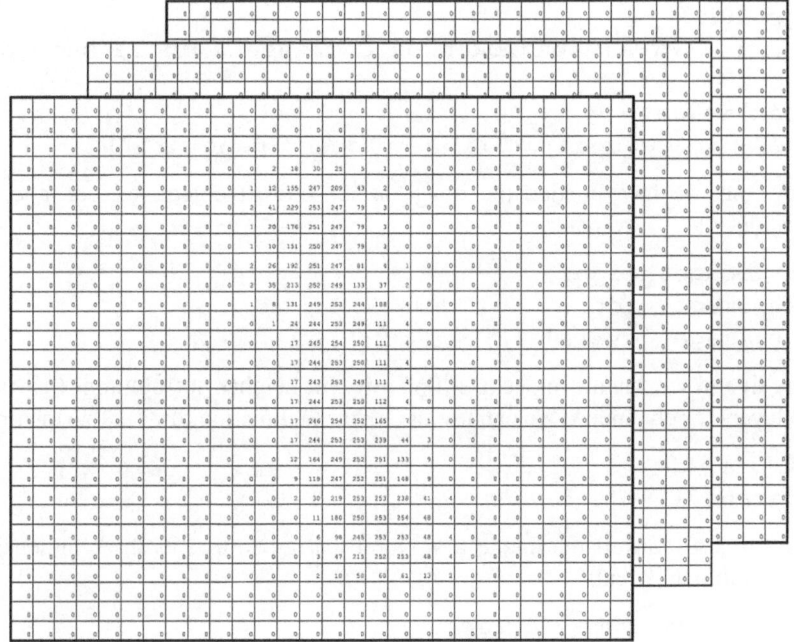

Fig. 13.2 Three-channel image

13.1.2 Reading Images in Python

Now that you know how images are stored, we will show how to load an image in Python. The libraries that we will use in this section are OpenCV (`pip install opencv-python`); the Python Imaging Library, also known as Pillow (`pip install pillow`); and NumPy, which you should already have installed. We will also use `urllib` for convenience.

image_example.py:

```
1  import cv2
2  import numpy as np
3
4  from PIL import Image
5  from urllib.request import urlopen
```

The image we will work with in this section is one of the most iconic political images in history: J. M. Flagg's 1917 "Uncle Sam" poster. The `Image` class in the Pillow library provides a nice interface for opening images. It will determine the format from the filename, so we can easily work with a variety of supported image formats.

```
 7 image_url =
     "http://www.mattdickenson.com/assets/uncle-sam.jpg"
 8
 9 # Load image
10 image = Image.open(urllib2.urlopen(image_url))
```

Now that we have loaded the image as an Image object, we can check its dimensions:

```
12 print(image.height)
13 print(image.width)
14 print(image.layers)
```

You should see that the image has 1062 rows (its height), 800 columns (its width), and 3 layers (or channels). We can use the show() function to visualize the image:

```
16 # Display image
17 image.show()
```

We can also convert the image to a NumPy array so that its three-dimensional nature is more apparent:

```
19 # Convert to Numpy array
20 image_array = np.array(image)
21 print(image_array.shape)
```

The OpenCV library makes it straightforward to convert between color spaces, such as converting the image to grayscale. The color conversion (cvtColor) function takes an NumPy array and a conversion as input, and returns a NumPy array. Notice that this reduces the number of channels from three to one (Fig. 13.3).

```
23 # Convert to greyscale
24 grey_image_array = cv2.cvtColor(image_array,
       cv2.COLOR_RGB2GRAY)
25 print(grey_image_array.shape)
```

If we wish to display the greyscale image with the Image.show() function we used above, we must convert it back to an Image object. It is also straightforward to save the image, with the format inferred from the filename string.

```
27 # Convert back to an Image object and display
28 grey_image = Image.fromarray(grey_image_array)
29 grey_image.show()
30 grey_image.save("greyscale.jpg")
```

Fig. 13.3 Color conversion example

13.1.3 Feature Extraction

Now that we have loaded the data we can begin to think about how to conduct our analysis. To do so, we want to derive features that are both tractable and interpretable. How can we extract such features for our analysis?

As you saw in the example of a binary image above, images contain a great deal of redundant or superfluous information. Converting an image from a 28-by-28 pixel MNIST image to a classification of the digit it represents will result in a massive reduction in dimensionality: from $2^{(28 \times 28)}$ possible binary images to 10 possible output classes (the digits 0–9). If we wished to use the 28-by-28 binary image in a conventional tabular analysis we would have to represent the pixels with 768 individual columns. Furthermore, doing this would discard the spatial information present in the image.

To overcome this challenge, image analysis requires one or more *feature extraction* steps to convert the image into scalar values. For example, we could use an edge detector to count the number of edges in an image. Similarly, we could use a sliding window to count how many patches in an image were of a certain color. These operations are known as *convolutions*.

Although a thorough discussion of useful convolutions is beyond the scope of this text, you should understand two things about them. First, there are many possible convolutions that can be applied to an image depending on the features you are interested in. Second (and as a result of the first point), using machine learning to automatically extract important features has become so popular that convolutions have lent their name to one of the most important methods in contemporary computer vision: convolutional neural networks. These are the types of models employed by the third-party computer vision APIs listed above that we recommend as a starting point for more advanced research involving image data.[11]

In this section, we will provide a simple example of feature extraction. For the image we loaded above, how many pixels are red, blue, and green, respectively? This technique could be used to answer research questions such as whether Democratic campaign ads contain more blue and Republican ads contain more red (the colors commonly associated with each party).

Using the NumPy array that we already created, we can easily compute which channel has the greatest pixel value for each pixel with the `argmax` function:

```
32 # Feature extraction
33 max_channels = np.argmax(image_array, axis=2)
```

Now we can compute the count for each color using the channel ordering (RGB):

```
35 red_count = max_channels[max_channels==0].size
36 blue_count = max_channels[max_channels==1].size
37 green_count = max_channels[max_channels==2].size
38 print("Red: {} Blue: {} Green: {}".format(red_count,
       blue_count, green_count))
```

Of course, if we were comparing multiple images of different sizes, we would need to account for the dimensions to make the figures comparable for each image. Here we compute the proportion of the image best represented by each color:

```
40 # Convert to proportion
41 num_pixels = max_channels.shape[0] *
       max_channels.shape[1]
42 red_prop = red_count / num_pixels
43 blue_prop = blue_count / num_pixels
44 green_prop = green_count / num_pixels
45 print("Red: {} Blue: {} Green: {}".format(red_prop,
       blue_prop, green_prop))
```

Do these results surprise you? In an image that appears to the naked eye as consisting almost exclusively of red, white, and blue pixels, the channel with highest intensity for about 18% of the pixels is green, while blue is the highest intensity value for less than 3% of the pixels. We can conduct a sanity check on this by plotting each channel separately as a greyscale image.

Figure 13.4 shows each channel one at a time. By comparing the second and third panes, you can see that most of the pixels that appear as blue in the original

---

[11] For one of the best contemporary introductions to convolutional neural networks, see http://cs231n.github.io/convolutional-networks/.

13.2 Nighttime Lights and Population

Fig. 13.4 Image decomposed to RGB channels

image actually have higher intensity values of green. If you were to conduct a wider analysis of campaign advertisements as suggested above, you would have to account for details like this that are not immediately obvious until you inspect the data yourself.

Now that you understand how image data is stored and how to work with it in Python, the next section provides a deeper dive into an example research question. The analysis below uses imagery in TIF format, but many of the same principles apply. The main difference is the spatial nature of the imagery, so we show how to convert between spatial and pixel coordinates.

13.2 Nighttime Lights and Population

To demonstrate the use of visual data for political research, this section investigates whether nighttime light data extracted from satellite imagery is a reliable proxy for population estimates. We show how to obtain publicly available image data, extract regions of interest, derive features, and use them in a quantitative analysis.

13.2.1 Nighttime Lights Data

As of August, 2017, there were 1738 operational satellites orbiting the Earth [4]. Of these, 620 serve observation-related purposes: capturing data for meteorological, environmental, and other scientific purposes. About half of these observational satellites (379) capture some form of imagery (optical, radar, or infrared). Because any individual satellite can only observe a fraction of the Earth's surface at any point in time, obtaining global coverage often requires operating groups of satellites as a system.

One such observational system is the Joint Polar Satellite System (JPSS), operated by the U.S. National Oceanic and Atmospheric Administration (NOAA) in partnership with the U.S. National Aeronautics and Space Administration (NASA).[12] One of the sensors included in this program is the Visible Infrared Imaging Radiometer Suite (VIIRS). VIIRS sensors capture 22 bands of the electromagnetic spectrum and can be used for environmental purposes such as cloud coverage, sea surface temperature, surface ice, and vegetation [1].

The imagery bands that we are concerned with for this project are the Day/Night Bands (DNB), which capture levels of nighttime light around the world at a 750-m resolution (i.e., one pixel in an image corresponds to a 750-by-750 meter grid square). This data is available at a daily granularity[13] but for this analysis we will use the monthly cloud-free composites.[14] These composites include corrections for cloud coverage and stray light, but can still suffer from seasonal effects such as illumination at the north and south poles during their respective summer months. In this project we will examine regions of the contiguous U.S., so these polar regions are outside the scope of our analysis.

To project the (approximately) spherical Earth into flat images, VIIRS data products are presented as six image tiles: three each north and south of the equator, each covering 120° of latitude. Data for North America can be found in Tile 1, which covers the region from 75° north to the equator and from 180° to 60° west latitude. We will use imagery from January, 2016, shown in thumbnail form below (Fig. 13.5).

13.2.2 Population Estimates

The U.S. performs a full census every 10 years, but the U.S. Census Bureau also releases annual updates. These updates are estimates of the change in population due to births, deaths, and migration. At the time of writing, the most recently released population estimates are for the year ending July 1, 2016.[15] The satellite imagery data from January 2016 described above aligns with the midpoint of the estimated population for this period.

As you can see, the daily and monthly availability of nighttime lights data is considerably more granular than a decennial census or even annual population estimates. If our analysis shows that nighttime lights data is an accurate proxy for

---

[12] For information on this program's European counterpart, the European Space Research Institute (ESRI), see http://www.esa.int/About_Us/ESRIN.

[13] See ftp://ftp-npp.class.ngdc.noaa.gov/.

[14] https://www.ngdc.noaa.gov/eog/viirs/download_dnb_composites.html.

[15] See https://www.census.gov/programs-surveys/popest/data/tables.2016.html.

13.2 Nighttime Lights and Population

Fig. 13.5 VIIRS DNB Tile 1, January 2016

population, this would give social scientists the ability to operate on more recent and more frequently updated figures. Nighttime lights data could also inform population estimates in regions where census data is unavailable or unreliable.[16]

13.2.3 Code Walk-through

Our project will consist of three steps: downloading data, preprocessing the data to extract features, and analysis. We will organize the data for this project in a subdirectory called "imagery" (though of course in your own code you can call it something else if you prefer). The code will be separated into three files–fetch_data.py, preprocessing.py, and analysis.py–each corresponding to one stage of the project. We will show how to share code between these stages so that information such as the location of data is not duplicated between them.

This analysis will use the 35 largest U.S. cities by population (ranging from New York City with a population of over eight million to Sacramento, California, with a population of just under 500,000). Although these cities constitute a biased sample of U.S. metropolitan areas, they offer a geographically diverse set of regions.

13.2.3.1 Retrieving Data

The first step in this analysis is to download copies of the data described above. The first file (SVDNB_npp_20160101-20160131_75N180W_vcmcfg_v10_

---

[16]For example, Lebanon has not conducted an official census since 1932 for political reasons that are beyond the scope of this text [7].

c201603132032.avg_rade9h.tif) should be retrieved from the Harvard Dataverse at https://dataverse.harvard.edu/dataset.xhtml?persistentId=doi%3A10.7910%2FDVN%2FTH3VW4.[17]

We will use the wget package (pip install wget) to simplify the download process.

At the beginning of our script, we import the packages we need and set up constants (shown in uppercase letters to distinguish them from variables) indicating both the remote and local file locations:

fetch_data.py:

```
 1  import csv
 2  import os
 3  import json
 4  import tarfile
 5  import googlemaps
 6  import wget
 7
 8  # Set filenames to be shared by other scripts
 9  TIF_PATH =
        'SVDNB_npp_20160101-20160131_75N180W_vcmcfg_v10_
        c201603132032.' + \
10      'avg_rade9h.tif'
11  CENSUS_CSV_URL =
        'https://www2.census.gov/programs-surveys/popest/'
        + \
12                  'datasets/2010-2016/' + \
13                  'cities/totals/sub-est2016_all.csv'
14  CENSUS_CSV_PATH = CENSUS_CSV_URL.split('/')[-1]
15  CITY_CSV_URL =
        'https://gist.githubusercontent.com/mcdickenson/' +
        \
16              '461961f337d2b9e165cbe0abc14e15f8/raw/'
        + \
17
        '13b7f0c182bb09187bb92f2c4fde27c683bdf455/city_
        codes.csv'
```

In addition to the VIIRS data (TARFILE_PATH) and the census population estimates (CENSUS_CSV_URL), we list two helper files. The first (CITY_CSV_URL) is a mapping between place names and the state, county, and place codes used in the census data. The second (GEOCODES_PATH) will be used to store geographic locations of the cities that we will obtain by geocoding them with the Google Maps API that you used in Chap. 7.

---

[17] Since the original draft of our manuscript, they were removed from the NOAA website. We have placed these files in the Dataverse for reproducibility.

13.2 Nighttime Lights and Population

Since we will be downloading several files, we also include a helper function to simplify this process and reduce the amount of repetition in the script:

fetch_data.py:

```
19  GEOCODES_PATH = 'geocodes.json'
20
21  def download_file(path, url):
```

Notice that this function will only download a file from a URL if the destination path does not already exist. This serves two purposes. First, it keeps us from accidentally overwriting the files. Second, it helps to make our code *idempotent*: the code can be run repeatedly while producing the same result, and it will not use more network bandwidth than necessary. Both of these characteristics help to make our analysis reproducible by other researchers.

We also add two more helper functions that will be used in both this file and later in our analysis:

fetch_data.py:

```
24
25
26  # make a coordinates file and geocode each city
27  def load_cities():
28      geoids = {}
29      with open(CITY_CSV_PATH, 'r') as csvfile:
30          csv_reader = csv.DictReader(csvfile)
31          for row in csv_reader:
32              city = row['city']
33              state = row['state']
34              city_state = '{}, {}'.format(city, state)
35              geoids[city_state] = {
36                  'state': row['state_code'],
37                  'county': row['county_code'],
38                  'place': row['place_code']
39              }
40
41      cities = geoids.keys()
42      return cities, geoids
43
44
45  def load_geocodes(cities):
46      if os.path.exists(GEOCODES_PATH):
47          with open(GEOCODES_PATH, 'r') as geocode_file:
48              geocodes = json.loads(geocode_file.read())
49      else:
50          api_key = os.getenv('GOOGLE_MAPS_API_KEY')
51          gmaps = googlemaps.Client(key=api_key)
```

```
52
53          geocodes = {}
54          for city in cities:
55              print("Geocoding {}".format(city))
56              geocode_result = gmaps.geocode(city)
57              location =
        geocode_result[0]['geometry']['location']
58              geocodes[city] = location
59
60          with open(GEOCODES_PATH, 'w') as geocode_file:
61              geocode_file.write(json.dumps(geocodes))
```

The `load_cities` function provides a nice interface for working with the city name-to-place code mapping that we described above. It will open the CSV file, iterate over it, and store a mapping from the city and state name to its census place codes. Notice that the function returns two values: a list of city names, and the name-to-place code mapping.

The `load_geocodes` function is another example of idempotency: the first time we run it, it will save its results to a file. Every time after that, the results will be loaded from the cache file instead of fetched again from the Google Maps API. Again, this makes your analysis reproducible and saves resources.

This function iterates over a list of city names, calls the Google Maps geocoding API, and extracts the latitude and longitude for the city center. When running this code, be sure to replace the value of the `api_key` variable with the same API key that you used in Chap. 7. You could do this by setting an environment variable, or by editing the code directly and putting your key in as a string. However, you should be careful not to share your code publicly (e.g., in a public GitHub repo) since then it could be used by others without your permission.

Now that we are done defining constants and helper functions, we turn to the running portion of the script:

fetch_data.py:

```
63      return geocodes
64
65  if __name__ == "__main__":
66      # Setup the working directory
67      if not os.path.exists('imagery'):
68          os.mkdir('imagery')
69
70      os.chdir('imagery')
71
72      # ensure that imagery is present
73      if not os.path.exists(TIF_PATH):
74          raise Exception("Download %s from the
        Dataverse".format(TIF_PATH))
75
```

13.2 Nighttime Lights and Population

```
76      # download census population estimates
77      download_file(CENSUS_CSV_PATH, CENSUS_CSV_URL)
78
79      # download mapping between city names and Census
            Bureau codes
80      download_file(CITY_CSV_PATH, CITY_CSV_URL)
81
82      # load city data and geocodes
83      cities, geoids = load_cities()
84      geocodes = load_geocodes(cities)
```

Nesting this portion of our script under the clause **if __name__ ...** ensures that this behavior only occurs when the script is run from the command line. In later stages of our analysis we will be importing our `fetch_data` script to get access to the constants and helper functions. However, we do not need the downloads to occur every time we import the file, so we nest them under this clause to ensure that they only run when we intend them to.

This portion of the script ensures that the `imagery` subdirectory exists, and sets it as the working directory (`os.chdir()`) so that all the downloaded files are located at that path. Since the VIIRS data is only available in the form of a tarfile (similar to a `.zip` file), we also have to extract the contents. Finally, we geocode each city and save the latitude and longitude of its center in our `geocodes.json` file.

After running this file to obtain the data, you are ready to proceed to the preprocessing step.

13.2.3.2 Preprocessing and Feature Extraction

Now that we have obtained the VIIRS nighttime lights data and population estimates, how do we prepare them for our analysis? In this section we will show how to process the imagery data to extract regions of interest, derive features related to nighttime radiance, and store these features in a format that will lend itself to tabular analysis in the next subsection.

Again we begin by importing modules we will need. Two of these (Matplotlib and NumPy) you should have already installed when working through the code in previous chapters. We will use the `rasterio` package (`pip install rasterio`) to work with the TIF imagery. Recall that TIF files can also contain information about the spatial project in the data. Because we will have to convert coordinates between spatial regions (latitude and longitude) and pixels, we will use the `affine` package to handle these transformations.

preprocessing.py:

```
1  # Preprocessing: geocode each city and extract
       radiance information
2  import csv
```

```
 3  import os
 4  import matplotlib.pyplot as plt
 5  import numpy as np
 6  import rasterio
 7
 8  from fetch_data import CITY_CSV_PATH, CENSUS_CSV_PATH,
        TIF_PATH, \
 9          load_cities, load_geocodes
10  from affine import Affine
11
12  PROCESSED_DATA_CSV_PATH = 'population_radiance.csv'
```

In addition to importing the external packages we need, we also import the helper functions and constants that we defined in fetch_data.py. This ensures that we are operating on the same paths across both files, and keeps us from having to update our code in multiple places if one of these paths changes. We also set up a new constant indicating the name of the final file that our preprocessing script will generate.

Next, we define a helper function that will convert from a region defined in latitude–longitude coordinates to a bounding box in pixel space. Our function will default to region of 2° longitude by 0.5° latitude. We could also extract regions using shapefiles for the metro areas in our analysis, but this would be somewhat more complicated and could bias our results due to different region sizes. Using boxes of the same size for every city ensures that we are operating on the same number of underlying pixels.[18]

```
14  def bbox_from_lat_long(lat, lng, lng_diff=1,
        lat_diff=0.25):
15      ymin = lat - lat_diff
16      ymax = lat + lat_diff
17      xmin = lng - lng_diff
18      xmax = lng + lng_diff
19      col_start, row_start = ~aff * (xmin, ymax)
20      col_stop, row_stop = ~aff * (xmax, ymin)
21      return ((int(row_start), int(row_stop)),
            (int(col_start), int(col_stop)))
```

This function used the inverse of the affine transformation (~aff) stored in the TIF file (loaded below) to convert from spatial to pixel coordinates. It returns a four-element tuple indicating the bounding box representing by pixel indexes.

Everything else in this script will be run inside another if __name__ == "__main__" block as we explained in the previous section. First, we set our

---

[18] Unfortunately, the bounding boxes Dallas–Fort Worth and San Francisco–San Jose do overlap. For a more robust version of this analysis, you could exclude one or both of the overlapping cities, or use a smaller region.

13.2 Nighttime Lights and Population

working directory and load a list of 480-by-120 pixel sub-images (also known as "snippets").

```
24  if __name__ == "__main__":
25      os.chdir('imagery')
26
27      # Load snippets for each city
28      cities, geo_ids = load_cities()
29      geocodes = load_geocodes(cities)
30      sub_images = {}
31      with rasterio.open(TIF_PATH) as src:
32          aff = src.affine
33          for city in cities:
34              print("processing {}".format(city))
35              geo = geocodes[city]
36              bbox = bbox_from_lat_long(geo['lat'],
     geo['lng'])
37              arr = src.read(1, window=bbox)
38              sub_images[city] = arr
```

This portion of the script reuses the geocode data that we collected in the previous section, so that the latitude and longitude of each city center serves as the centroid of the region of interest. The snippets are loaded into a list for use below.

Before extracting features from this data, it is a good idea to visualize the imagery to ensure that it looks as expected. We will bucket the radiances into percentiles so that bright areas show up as red, moderately lit areas as yellow, and dark areas as blue.

```
42      if not os.path.exists('fig-full.png'):
43          percs = [x*10 for x in range(11)]
44          fig, ax = plt.subplots(nrows=7, ncols=5,
     figsize=(40, 20))
45
46          for ix, city in enumerate(cities):
47              row = int(ix / 5)
48              col = ix % 5
49              a = ax[row][col]
50              arr = sub_images[city]
51              print("{}: {}".format(city, arr.shape))
52              bins = [np.percentile(arr, p) for p in
     percs]
53              dig = np.digitize(arr, bins, right=False)
54              a.imshow(dig)
55              a.text(0, 120, city, color='white')
56              a.get_xaxis().set_visible(False)
57              a.get_yaxis().set_visible(False)
```

Fig. 13.6 Nighttime lights data for major U.S. cities

```
58         fig.subplots_adjust(wspace=0, hspace=0)
59         fig.savefig('fig-full.png')
```

The snippets are displayed in a 7-by-5 grid in descending order of population. We save the final result as a PNG image, displayed in Fig. 13.6.

You can perform a sanity check on this data using your knowledge of U.S. cities. Notice that inland cities (San Antonio, Denver) often expand in a hub-and-spoke pattern symmetrically from their center, while coastal cities (Los Angeles, Seattle) have their population centers along the coast and the population gradient descends as you move inland. The relative size of the cities is also somewhat evident at a first glance, with most metro areas larger than El Paso extending a bit beyond the bounding box and smaller cities being easily contained within it.

Now we are ready to extract radiance information as a feature that can be easily used in a tabular analysis. Here we will use the average pixel value within the bounding box as a proxy for nighttime illumination. You could easily extract other features—percentiles, variance, or standard deviation—for your own further analysis.

```
65  geo_ids_inverted = {"{}-000-{}".format(v['state'],
        v['place']): k \
66                      for k, v in geo_ids.items()}
67
68      data = {}
69
70      # read population data
71      with open(CENSUS_CSV_PATH, 'r',
            encoding="ISO-8859-1") as csvfile:
72          csv_reader = csv.DictReader(csvfile)
```

13.2 Nighttime Lights and Population

```
73          for row in csv_reader:
74              place = str(row['PLACE'])
75              state = str(row['STATE'])
76              county = str(row['COUNTY'])
77              key = "{}-{}-{}".format(state, county, place)
78              if key not in geo_ids_inverted.keys():
79                  continue
80              city = geo_ids_inverted[key]
81              data[city] = {'population': row['POPESTIMATE2016']}
82
83
84      # write data to csv
85      with open(PROCESSED_DATA_CSV_PATH, 'w') as f:
86          csv_writer = csv.DictWriter(f, fieldnames=('city', 'population', 'avg_radiance'))
87          csv_writer.writeheader()
88          for city, data_points in data.items():
89              row = data_points
90              row['city'] = city
91              arr = sub_images[city]
92              row['avg_radiance'] = np.mean(arr)
93              csv_writer.writerow(row)
```

We load the population data first, and store it in our `data` dictionary. Then, we iterate over the cities, compute our feature extraction `np.mean()`, and write the result to our CSV file. The result is a file with three columns as shown below.

```
1 city,population,avg_radiance
2 "Charlotte, NC",842051,5.26974
3 "Tucson, AZ",530706,1.69711
4 ...
5 "Houston, TX",2303482,16.0838
```

Once you have run this preprocessing code and have your output stored in the `population_radiance.csv` file, you are ready to move on to the final step in this analysis.

13.2.3.3 Analysis

The `analysis.py` script will begin in the same way as `fetch_data.py` and `preprocessing.py`: with importing packages and constants.

analysis.py:

```
1  import os
2  import matplotlib.pyplot as plt
3  import numpy as np
4  import pandas as pd
5  from sklearn import linear_model
6
7  from preprocessing import PROCESSED_DATA_CSV_PATH
```

Again, you should already have installed these packages when working through previous chapters. If not, all of them can be installed with `pip`.

Next, we set our working directory, read in the CSV file, and look at its first few lines to ensure that it was loaded correctly:

```
10 os.chdir('imagery')
11
12 # Load data
13 data = pd.read_csv(PROCESSED_DATA_CSV_PATH)
14
15 print(data.head())
```

Once the data is loaded in a data frame, create a scatterplot with radiance on the *x*-axis and population on the y-axis (Fig. 13.7).

```
17 # Visualizing data
18 fig = plt.figure()
19 plt.scatter(data['avg_radiance'], data['population'])
20 plt.xlabel('Avg Radiance')
```

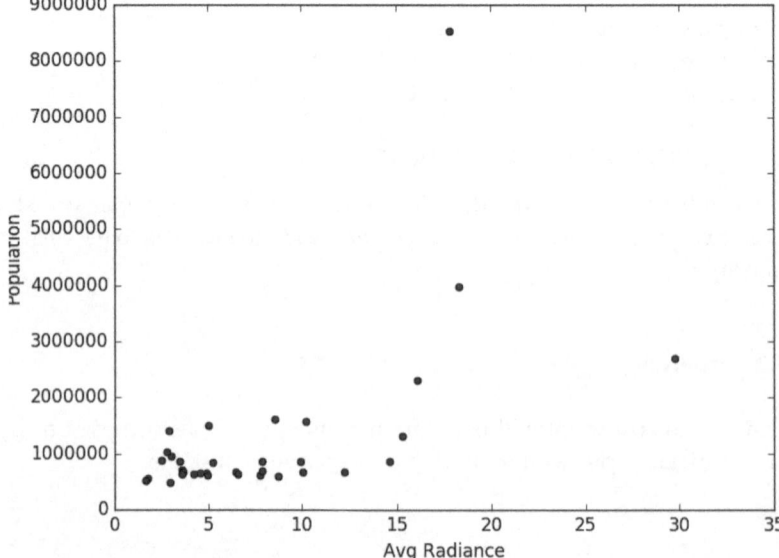

Fig. 13.7 Radiance and population, linear scale

13.2 Nighttime Lights and Population

```
21 plt.ylabel('Population')
22 fig.savefig("graph1.png")
```

Notice the obvious outlier in this data: New York City has a much larger population than even the second largest U.S. city, Los Angeles. This visualization suggests that we should work with population data in log-scaled units. To do this, we compute an auxiliary column in our data frame and plot it again:

```
25 data['log_pop'] = np.log(data['population'])
26
27 fig = plt.figure()
28 plt.scatter(data['avg_radiance'], data['log_pop'])
29 plt.xlabel('Avg Radiance')
30 plt.ylabel('Population (logged)')
31 fig.savefig("graph2.png")
```

When viewed on a log scale, it begins to look as if there may be a linear relationship between nighttime radiance and population. To analyze this quantitatively, we will fit a linear regression (ordinary least-squares) model to this data (Fig. 13.8).[19]

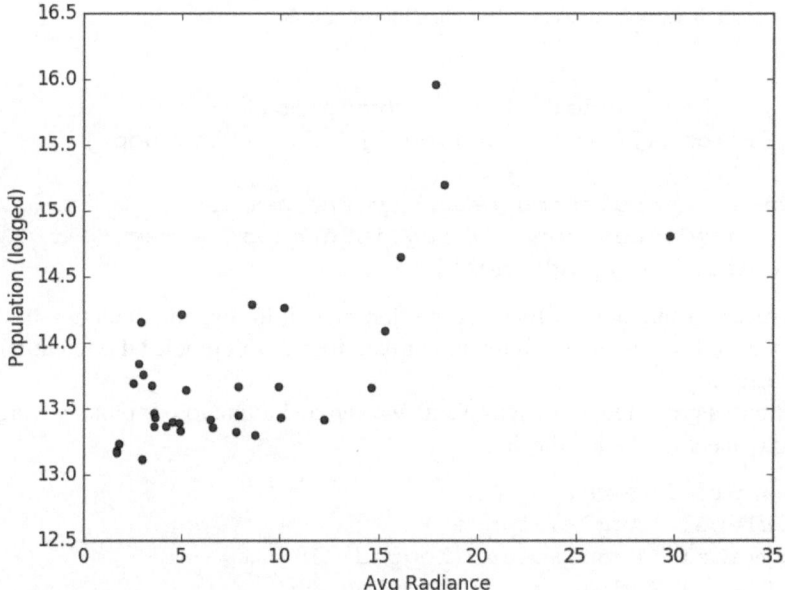

Fig. 13.8 Radiance and population, log scale

---

[19] A thorough treatment of linear regression is beyond the scope of this chapter. See the "Further Reading" section for a list of useful introductory texts aimed at social scientists.

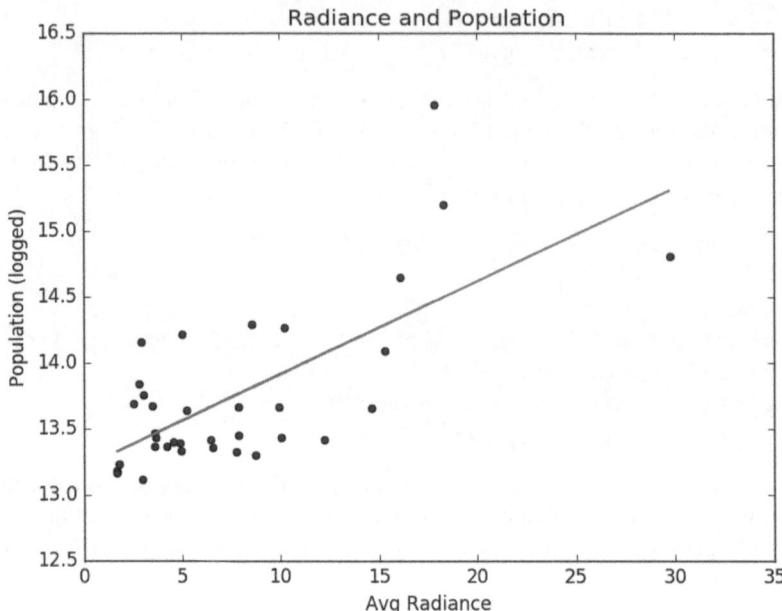

Fig. 13.9 Radiance and population, including line of best fit

```
34 reg = linear_model.LinearRegression()
35 reg.fit(data[['avg_radiance']], data['log_pop'])
36
37 # predict population based on the model
38 data['predicted_pop'] = reg.intercept_ + reg.coef_[0]
      * data['avg_radiance']
```

Here we instantiate our linear regression model, fit logged population based on radiance, and add another column to our data frame with predicted population (still on a log scale).

With this predicted column in place, we can add a line to our plot showing how well the linear model fits the data:

```
41 fig = plt.figure()
42 plt.xlabel('Avg Radiance')
43 plt.ylabel('Population (logged)')
44 plt.title('Radiance and Population')
45 plt.scatter(data['avg_radiance'], data['log_pop'])
46 plt.plot(data['avg_radiance'], data['predicted_pop'],
      'r')
47 plt.show()
48 fig.savefig("graph3.png")
```

Although there are still a few outliers lying some distance from the line of best fit, this indicates that nighttime radiance is a useful predictor for population levels (Fig. 13.9).

13.2.4 Results

In the preceding section you were able to obtain, process, and analyze visual data to investigate a social question: to what degree is nighttime lights data correlated with population? The model that we fit during our analysis showed that there is a strong linear relationship ($p < 0.001$, $R^2 = 0.475$) between average nighttime radiance and logged population estimates.

These results show that nighttime imagery data is a useful proxy for population. Moreover, this analysis demonstrates that there is a valuable place for image processing in a social scientist's toolkit. The final section of this chapter describes more advanced applications of computer vision and lists other avenues for applying imagery to social and political research questions.

13.3 Additional Applications and Further Reading

This chapter introduced the core concepts associated with image data, demonstrated how to work with satellite imagery, and described advanced computer vision applications. Now that you are familiar with how images are stored and processed, you can begin working with other sources of imagery. Satellite imagery is one of the most directly applicable image types for political analysis, and as more and more image datasets become available researchers will be empowered to use them to answer new and interesting questions. Furthermore, publicly accessible APIs such as Google Cloud Vision, Amazon Rekognition, and Microsoft Azure allow researchers to use state-of-the-art computer vision methods such as high-accuracy optical character recognition (OCR) processors.

With these skills in place, what questions might you attempt to answer using image data? You could begin by expanding on the nighttime lights analysis presented here. For example, is there seasonality associated with radiance levels? Are other seasonal trends, such as the north–south migration of retirees ("snowbirds") visible in the data? Does the level of radiance in a congressional district predict the characteristics or behavior of its representative?

You could also go beyond the U.S. to examine these and similar questions in an international context. Is economic activity predicted by the level of radiance of a country (or its capital city)? How is electrification tied to electoral politics [8]? Can satellite imagery measure levels of state control in conflict settings [5]? Is satellite data useful for assessing questions of decentralized governance in developing countries [6]?

Other forms of imagery could lend themselves to social science research questions as well. Recent research has shown that the types of vehicles observed in Google Street View images strongly correlate with social traits such as income, race, and voting patterns [2]. Crowd size estimation techniques could be used to obtain approximate attendance at protests or other political events.[20] Detection of particular objects in images (such as small arms weaponry) posted on social media services could also provide data about the evolution of conflict in urban areas such as Baghdad or Kiev.

For more information about the topics presented in this chapter, we recommend the following resources:

- Prince, S. J. (2012). *Computer vision: Models, learning, and inference.* Cambridge, UK: Cambridge University Press. This text is an excellent introduction to image processing and computer vision techniques.
- Goodfellow, I., Bengio, Y., & Courville, A. (2016). *Deep learning.* Cambridge, MA: MIT Press. The best text on deep learning, the current state-of-the-art for computer vision, by some of the leaders in the field.
- Solem, J. E. (2012). *Programming computer vision with Python: Tools and algorithms for analyzing images.* Sebastopol, CA: O'Reilly. Practical introduction to image processing techniques, a good starting place for readers of this text.
- Szeliski, R. (2010). *Computer vision: Algorithms and applications.* Berlin, DE: Springer Science & Business Media. Very thorough introduction to computer vision for readers interested in a deeper understanding of the concepts introduced in this chapter.
- Gill, J. (2000). *Generalized linear models: A unified approach.* Thousand Oaks, CA: Sage Publications. Introductory linear regression text aimed at social scientists.
- Gelman, A., & Hill, J. (2007). *Data analysis using regression and multilevel hierarchical models.* Cambridge, UK: Cambridge University Press. Very thorough introduction to linear regression and related models for social analysis.

References

1. Cao, C., Xiong, J., Blonski, S., Liu, Q., Uprety, S., Shao, X., ... & Weng, F. (2013). Suomi NPP VIIRS sensor data record verification, validation, and long-term performance monitoring. *Journal of Geophysical Research: Atmospheres, 118*(20), 11–664.
2. Gebru, T., et al. (2017). Using deep learning and Google Street View to estimate the demographic makeup of neighborhoods across the United States. *Proceedings of the National Academy of Sciences.* https://doi.org/10.1073/pnas.1700035114
3. Troy, G. (2005). The Living Room Candidate: Presidential Campaign Commercials, 1952–2004.

---

[20]Recall the controversy in the U.S. regarding attendance at the 2017 inauguration of Donald Trump [10].

References

4. Grimwood, T. (2017). UCS satellite database. https://www.ucsusa.org/nuclear-weapons/space-weapons/satellite-database. Cited 24 Mar 2018.
5. Hollenbach, F. M., Wibbels, E., & Michael, D. W. (2013). State building and the geography of governance: Evidence from satellites. Duke Ward Lab. http://citeseerx.ist.psu.edu/viewdoc/download?doi=10.1.1.712.3739. Cited 24 Mar 2018.
6. Huntington, H., & Wibbels, E. (2014). The geography of governance in Africa: New tools from satellites, surveys and mapping initiatives. *Regional & Federal Studies, 24*(5), 625–645.
7. Jerven, M. (2013). *Poor numbers: How we are misled by African development statistics and what to do about it.* Ithaca: Cornell University Press.
8. Min, B. (2015). *Power and the vote: Elections and electricity in the developing world.* Cambridge: Cambridge University Press.
9. Schill, D. (2012). The visual image and the political image: A review of visual communication research in the field of political communication. *Review of Communication, 12*(2), 118–142.
10. Wallace, T., Yourish, K., & Griggs, T. (2017). Trump's inauguration vs. Obama's: Comparing the crowds. https://www.nytimes.com/interactive/2017/01/20/us/politics/trump-inauguration-crowd.html. Cited 24 Mar 2018.

Chapter 14
Case Study: Natural Language Processing

This chapter will introduce concepts and techniques for using unstructured text as a data source. We will first review examples of the types of extant text data that you may encounter. We will then discuss the process of turning that text into a data source more amenable to the types of quantitative analysis that we are likely to perform.

We will then work through an example that uses social media data to estimate the party of political candidates. Specifically, there are patterns in the language of their Twitter communications that can accurately predict a US Senator's party.

Finally we will discuss further problems that may prove fertile ground for using these techniques.

The code in this chapter will also leverage several skills that you learned in earlier chapters, including file manipulation, API integration, and simple machine learning.

14.1 Working with Text Data

Textual data is everywhere. From the speeches that politicians give, to the content of social media we are surrounded by language. Language by its very nature encodes a lot of information—that is the whole point! Historically utilizing these data sources requires long hours of human coding. If we can leverage the language itself directly without using human intermediaries we can unlock large data streams that have been previously dismissed as intractable.

Electronic Supplementary Material The online version of this chapter (https://doi.org/10.1007/978-3-030-36826-5_14) contains supplementary material, which is available to authorized users.

The process of working with text as data is fundamentally no different than any other form of non-numeric data. The goal is to take the raw text and transform it into numeric format that is amenable to statistical analysis.

As you will see there are a number of decisions that are made during this process that are worth understanding. Most of them will focus on improving the signal-to-noise ratio in the corpus of text. Depending on your data sources and ultimate goals you may opt for different types of cleaning and transforming.

14.1.1 Text as Data

There are multiple ways to think about text as data and the correct form depends on your goals. While we will only cover a subset of the possible approaches in this case study they primarily break down into two types: metadata and content.

The metadata corresponding to a piece of text includes all of the attributes that are not actually derived from the texts' meaning. This includes things such as language, length, number of speakers, and time of creation. This type of information can often give important context to a statistical analysis, for example, if one were to analyze the Enron email corpus, understanding the sequence in which emails were sent and who sent them ("what did they know and when did they know it?") might be important.[2] This data is frequently already presented in either numerical or categorical form and ready for analysis.

The content of a textual corpus is captured by the words used. Transforming the content into usable material is where the vast majority of work in natural language processing takes place. There are a number of considerations when performing this transformation from handling inherently noisy data to normalization to how to define what words really mean.

When talking about content in this chapter we will describe a group of texts as a *corpus*. Each individual document will be called a text. Each word (or lemma) will be referred to as *token*. Finally, N contiguous tokens are referred to as an *n-gram*.

As of this writing, one of the most liked tweets on Twitter belongs to @BarackObama:

> ME: Joe, about halfway through the speech, I'm gonna wish you a happy birth– BIDEN: IT'S MY BIRTHDAY! ME: Joe.
> Happy birthday to @JoeBiden, my brother and the best vice president anybody could have. http://pic.twitter.com/sKbXjNiEjH

Metadata about this piece of text might include the fact that it was created on November 20, 2017. It was authored by Barack Obama. It has 227 characters and 35 tokens (words) of which 33 are unique.

The following techniques illustrate how to start turning this unstructured content into data.

---

[2]https://www.cs.cmu.edu/~enron/.

14.1.1.1 Cleanup

A lot of text, especially that from social media, contains content that does not add a lot of information. While it is always a judgment call for the researcher as to what content has a useful signal, it is very common to remove a number of classes of content from text before analyzing it.

Whitespace rarely adds any useful information to a statistical analysis and is frequently removed from a corpus:

```
def strip_whitespace(text):
    return text.strip().replace("\n", " ").replace("\r", " ")
```

URLs can be very difficult to aggregate as they look like unique tokens to many algorithms. It is common to remove URLs from text derived from social media, or at a minimum normalize them to just contain the domain.[3] For example, https://www.google.com/search?q=test might be normalized to www.google.com across an entire corpus. In our examples we will just remove all URLs:

```
def strip_urls(text):
    return re.sub(r'https?:\/\/\S*', '', text,
    flags=re.IGNORECASE)
```

Text artifacts are very common in text databases as a result of encoding issues (e.g., unicode to ASCII). Because in our example we will be pulling data from Twitter we should anticipate potential encoding problems coming from HTML:

```
def transform_html_entities(text):
    return text.replace("&amp;", "and").replace("&gt;", ">").replace("&lt;", "<")
```

If we perform the above to our starting tweet text we will get the following output:

> ME: Joe, about halfway through the speech, I'm gonna wish you a happy birth– BIDEN: IT'S MY BIRTHDAY! ME: Joe. Happy birthday to @JoeBiden, my brother and the best vice president anybody could have.

14.1.1.2 Normalization

After getting a baseline corpus of text that has had extraneous elements removed we turn to the task of normalizing the content.

---

[3]Part of the reason that they can be a bad signal is due to URL shorteners obfuscating the final destination.

There are a number of good tools for this including NLTK,[4] CoreNLP,[5] and others. We will be using spaCy, which you can install with `pip install spacy`.[6]

The goal of normalization during the NLP process is to collapse some of the nuance in spoken or written language and try to help strengthen the signal-to-noise ratio given our human knowledge about a specific language. To that end we will lemmatize, remove stop words and numbers/symbols to eliminate extraneous or low information portions of the text.

14.1.1.3 Lemmatization

Lemmatization is a technique for collapsing all of the various inflected forms of a word into a single item. This results in treating "walk," "walking," "walked," "walks," etc. as one token: "walk." The intuition behind why we do this is that all forms of the lemma are intended to convey the fundamental idea of *walking*. While our human brains know that, we need to capture that somehow in our dataset. The algorithms that will consume this text do not know that just because there is large character overlap, these words are variations of the same concept.

Lemmatization is different than *stemming* in two main ways. First lemmatization takes into account word meaning, instead of just grammatical rules. So "I went to the store" and "I will go to the store" will both lemmatize the verb to "go" where they would be stemmed to "went" and "go," respectively. Second, lemmatization will always result in a real word. So while the lemma for "ceased" is "cease," a stemmer would pick the non-word "ceas."

To handle this easily in our example we will take advantage of spaCy's built-in lemmatizer. Note that pronouns in this case are lemmatized to "-PRON-."

```
def lemmatize(tokens):
    lemmas = []
    for token in tokens:
        lemmas.append(token.lemma_.lower().strip() if
    token.lemma_ != "-PRON-" else token.lower_)

    return lemmas
```

14.1.1.4 Stop Words

Not all words are created equal for the purposes of statistical investigation. While we may use function words such as "the" or "at" to convey subtle meaning while

---
[4]https://www.nltk.org/.
[5]https://stanfordnlp.github.io/CoreNLP/.
[6]https://spacy.io/.

speaking, they are so common in almost any corpus of English text that their presence provides little differentiating information. Because of this, it is common practice in natural language processing to filter out stop words before performing any analysis. While there are no hard rules for which words are stop words, we will rely on spaCy's list to remove them from our text.

```
def strip_stopwords(tokens):
    tokens = [token for token in tokens if not
    token.is_stop]
    return tokens
```

14.1.1.5 Numbers and Symbols

Finally, numbers and symbols are commonly excluded as they are very frequent and typically present themselves as singletons in a corpus. To remove these we will only include tokens in our final cleaned set of words that are alphabetical.

```
def strip_symbols(tokens):
    tokens = [token for token in tokens if
    token.is_alpha]
    return tokens
```

If we run the above on our cleaned tweet we get the following final result:

me joe halfway speech i go to wish happy biden it my birthday me joe happy birthday brother well vice president anybody

While this is no longer grammatically correct it still captures much of the essence of the tweet.

14.1.2 Transformation

The final step before we begin performing analysis on our tweets is to turn the tokens into something numerical that we can analyze. We will discuss three common approaches to this problem, but note that this is an area of active research and we will just skim the surface of what is possible.

14.1.2.1 Count Vectorization

Count vectorization is the process of converting a corpus of documents into a matrix of token counts. The full set of possible tokens is called the *vocabulary* of the vectorization.

The matrix for a count vectorization will have one axis that represents all of the possible tokens (columns) and one axis (rows) that represents each document. The cells are filled with the number of times that the corresponding token appeared in the document. For corpuses with large vocabularies this is frequently a very sparse matrix.

In our tweet example the count vectorization might look like the following vector: $\begin{bmatrix} 1 & 1 & 2 & 1 & \ldots & 1 \end{bmatrix}$

where the vector indices correspond to the words in the vocabulary (unique tokens) alphabetically, i.e. (anybody, biden, birthday, brother ... wish).

14.1.2.2 TF-IDF Vectorization

TF-IDF Vectorization transforms words into a matrix that takes a similar form as a Count Vectorization, except the values in each cell are the term frequency-inverse document frequency values of each token [4]. This value increases with the number of appearances that a token makes in a document but decreases with the number of appearances that it makes in the overall corpus. Thus extremely common words will have a lower score, but a word that appears frequently in one document but infrequently everywhere else will have a high score for that document.

14.1.2.3 Word Embeddings

Most modern machine learning based approaches to NLP perform a slightly more complicated transformation. Word Embeddings are a set of techniques to map words or phrases from a vocabulary to real-numbered vectors. The goal is that words that share common meaning or context in the corpus should be close to one another in the vector space.

There are numerous approaches to creating word embeddings, the most popular of which, such as Word2Vec[2], can be obtained as pretrained models. When using pretrained models you can map the word or phrase directly into the vector space (spacy provides pretrained word embeddings) and utilize those in your models. Note that the optimal size of the vector space is frequently determined empirically.

14.2 Party and Social Media

To show that text is a valuable signal that can be used for statistical analysis, we will leverage a number of skills that have been developed over the course of this book. Our goal will be to determine whether the content of US Senators' tweets can accurately predict their party affiliation.

We will first get recent tweets from current senators. We will then preprocess the text and sanity check our hypothesis via some simple EDA. Finally we will see if we can predict a senator's party using only the content of their tweets.

14.2.1 US Senators' Tweets

We will start by utilizing Civil Service USA's Senate dataset.[7] They have helpfully compiled a number of useful attributes regarding each member of the 115th Senate into readily consumable datasets and made them available via an MIT license.[8] The one we are most interested in are: party and Twitter handle. The code in this section corresponds to the `fetch_data.py` file.

The process of loading and storing the data for each senator will look very similar to our previous work utilizing Twitter data. First, we will load the Senator dataset:

```
1  import tweepy
2  import pandas as pd
3  import sys, os
4  import re
5
6  CONSUMER_KEY       = 'XXX'
7  CONSUMER_SECRET    = 'XXX'
8  ACCESS_TOKEN       = 'XXX'
9  ACCESS_SECRET      = 'XXX'
10
11 SENATE_DATA_URL = 'https://raw.githubusercontent.com/
12     CivilServiceUSA/us-senate/master/us-senate/data/
13                  us-senate.csv'
14
15 DATA_FOLDER        = './datasets/'
16
17 def load_congressional_data():
18     # Load Congress social media data
19     senate_social_info = pd.read_csv(SENATE_DATA_URL)
20     senate_social_info.to_csv(DATA_FOLDER +
    'senate_social_info.csv')
21     return senate_social_info
```

Now that we have imported this into a pandas dataframe we can iterate over all of the senators and download their most recent tweets. The most recent tweets will assuredly not be the same at the time of this book's writing as at the time of its consumption so the exact data used in this exercise have been included with the book.

In the `pull_tweets` method, we create an authenticated Twitter client as in Chap. 7. We then load the most recent 200 tweets for each senator in the list. In the

---
[7] https://github.com/CivilServiceUSA/us-senate.
[8] If you wish to replicate this study exactly, the CSV version of the dataset is included with the book at https://dataverse.harvard.edu/dataverse/python-book.

existing dataset, one of the social media handles was incorrect, so we need to handle error cases throughout.

```
21  def pull_tweets(senate_social_info):
22      auth = tweepy.OAuthHandler(CONSUMER_KEY,
        CONSUMER_SECRET)
23      auth.set_access_token(ACCESS_TOKEN, ACCESS_SECRET)
24      api = tweepy.API(auth)
25
26      # Load and store
27      for ix, senator_info in
        senate_social_info.iterrows():
28          try:
29              filename = DATA_FOLDER +
        senator_info.bioguide + ".txt"
30
31              # Don't re-do work
32              if not os.path.isfile(filename):
33                  print("Loading tweets for " +
        senator_info.twitter_handle)
34                  senator_tweets =
        api.user_timeline(senator_info.twitter_handle,
        count=200)
35
36                  tweets = []
37                  for tweet in senator_tweets:
38                      tweets.append(tweet.text)
39
40                  with open(filename, 'w') as f:
41                      print("Saving tweets for " +
        senator_info.twitter_handle)
42
        f.write("\n".join(tweets).encode('ascii', 'ignore'))
43              else:
44                  print("Skipping tweets for " +
        senator_info.twitter_handle)
45
46          except Exception as e:
47              print(e)
48              print("Error saving tweets for " +
        senator_info.twitter_handle)
```

After executing `fetch_data.py` we now have individual text files with one tweet per line for each of the senators. The filenames uniquely identify the senator by their BioGuide ID.[9]

14.2.2 Tweet Normalization

Now that we have the raw tweets from each of the senators, we need to normalize the text as discussed in Sect. 14.1.1.1. While we have seen many of the normalization techniques before, an additional text cleanup action of removing "RT" (for retweet) was added, as in the Twitter context this functions as a stop word.

```
58  def strip_twitter_terms(text):
59      return re.sub(r'\brt', '', text,
        flags=re.IGNORECASE)
```

The final product of our preprocessing is a number of text files containing only the cleaned tokens for each senator.

```
58  def load_and_clean_tweets(senate_social_info):
59      senator_docs = []
60      for ix, senator_info in
        senate_social_info.iterrows():
61          filename = DATA_FOLDER + senator_info.bioguide
        + ".txt"
62          cleaned_filename = DATA_FOLDER + "cleaned-" +
        senator_info.bioguide + ".txt"
63          try:
64              print("Cleaning " + senator_info.last_name
        + " tweets.")
65              with open(filename, 'r') as f:
66                  tweets = f.read()
67                  cleaned_text = cleanup_text(tweets)
68                  doc = drop_oov_words(cleaned_text)
69              with open(cleaned_filename, 'w') as f:
70                  f.write(doc.text)
71          except:
72              print("ERROR: Cleaning " +
        senator_info.last_name + " tweets.")
73              pass
```

---

[9]https://www.congress.gov/help/field-values/member-bioguide-ids.

14.2.3 EDA

Now that we have a normalized dataset, we can start inspecting the data and seeing if our hypothesis that Democrats and Republicans are identifiable via their tweets seems plausible.

We can start by looking at the most frequently used words for each party. If our theory is true, we should expect to see a difference. To easily do this in Python we again will leverage spaCy but also textacy (pip install textacy) which provides helpful additional functionality to spaCy objects.[10]

```
20 senator_docs = []
21 for ix, senator_info in senate_social_info.iterrows():
22     filename = DATA_FOLDER + "cleaned-" +
       senator_info.bioguide + ".txt"
23     try:
24         with open(filename, 'r') as f:
25             tweets = f.read()
26             doc = nlp(tweets)
27             senator_docs.append({"text": doc, "party":
       senator_info.party, "name": senator_info.last_name})
28     except:
29         pass
30
31 republican_corpus = textacy.corpus.Corpus(nlp)
32 republican_corpus.add_docs([x['text'] for x in
       senator_docs if x['party'] == 'republican'])
33 democrat_corpus = textacy.corpus.Corpus(nlp)
34 democrat_corpus.add_docs([x['text'] for x in
       senator_docs if x['party'] == 'democrat'])
35
36 # Do the top word counts look different?
37 def top_word_list(corpus, top_words=15):
38     word_counts = corpus.word_freqs(weighting='count',
       as_strings=True)
39     return sorted(word_counts.items(), key=lambda x:
       x[1], reverse=True)[:top_words]
```

After loading our data, we split the data into two Corpus objects (these are textacy abstractions). We then print out the top words used in each corpus. The results look promising as the top 10 Republican words are:

- today
- senate

---

[10] https://github.com/chartbeat-labs/textacy.

14.2 Party and Social Media

- great
- thank
- work
- bill
- good
- meet
- hear
- join

Whereas the top 10 Democrat words are:

- today
- work
- trump
- thank
- new
- bill
- student
- great
- need
- help

While they have some overlap, note that the Republicans do not mention Trump or students as frequently as Democrats.

Another useful step is to use a dimensionality reduction technique to see if our categories are easily separated. In this example we perform a tSNE reduction[5] of the TF-IDF vectors for each Senator using the yellowbrick package (`pip install yellowbrick`). Note that at this point we remove the 2 independent senators from the corpus.

```
48 two_party_docs = [x for x in senator_docs if
      x['party'] in ['republican', 'democrat']]
49 vectorizer = TfidfVectorizer(min_df=3,
      max_features=500, ngram_range=(1,2), norm='l2',
      smooth_idf=True, sublinear_tf=False, use_idf=True)
50 X = vectorizer.fit_transform([x['text'].text for x in
      two_party_docs])
51 y = [x['party'] for x in two_party_docs]
52
53 tsne = TSNEVisualizer(random_state=8675309)
54 tsne.fit(X, y)
```

This results in the following plot, which shows very nice separation between the Democrats and Republicans. This should give us hope that there is some underlying latent dimension on which we can separate the two classes of senators (Fig. 14.1).

Fig. 14.1 tSNE reduction of TFIDF vectors

14.2.4 Results

Confident in the ability of the tweets to predict the party of the senators based on their tweets, we finally train a simple classifier. As this is a two category classification case and we are working with relatively few examples we start with a Linear Support Vector Classifier and assess its performance.

We begin by splitting our data into a train and a test set. We reserve one-third of the senators to test the accuracy of our classifier. To make any random division of your data replicable ensure that you specify a random state. We then vectorize the text by generating count vectors of length one n-grams and proceed to fit the model.

```
58 X = [x for x in two_party_docs]
59 y = [x['party'] for x in two_party_docs]
60 X_train, X_test, y_train, y_test = train_test_split(X,
      y, test_size=0.33, random_state=42)
61
62 vectorizer = CountVectorizer(ngram_range=(1,1))
63 classifier = LinearSVC()
64 pipe = Pipeline([('vectorizer', vectorizer),
65                  ('classifier', classifier)])
66
67 pipe.fit([x['text'].text for x in X_train], y_train)
```

With a fitted model we can now predict the party of the held back test set.

14.3 Additional Applications and Further Reading

```
70  pred_data = pipe.predict([x['text'].text for x in
        X_test])
71  print("Accuracy:", accuracy_score(y_test, pred_data))
72  print("Confusion:")
73  print(confusion_matrix(y_test, pred_data))
```

This very simple model, with no tuning, correctly predicts 94% of the unseen senators correctly! If we inspect the confusion matrix we can see that we correctly predicted all 17 Republican senators. We correctly predict 14 of 16 Democrat senators. To better understand our results lets try to identify which cases we missed.

```
76  for ix, x in enumerate(X_test):
77      wrong = "*" if y_test[ix] != pred_data[ix] else ""
78      print(wrong + y_test[ix] + "\t" + pred_data[ix] +
        "\t" + X_test[ix]['name'])
```

After running the above we can see that our classifier incorrectly identified Senators McCaskill and Manchin as Republican. Interestingly, both of these Senators are considered very moderate Democrats. The Washington Post ranked Senator McCaskill as the second most likely to vote against her party [3]. Senator Manchin has the highest NOMINATE score of any current Democratic senator [1].

So what can we conclude? Our very simple analysis should leave us confident that there is a strong signal in the social media presence of politicians. While this may not be a surprising result intuitively, we now have the skills to take a step toward proving it.

14.3 Additional Applications and Further Reading

Now that you are familiar with how to use text in statistical analyses where might you go from here? As we noted in the introduction, text data is ubiquitous, both in the form of spoken and transcribed language as well as written text. There is already a burgeoning literature taking advantage of these sources, from floor speeches, to campaign websites, to social media and beyond.

If we were to extend our example in this chapter you could consider the following questions:

- Do we believe these results? Can we improve the statistical robustness via cross-validation.
- How temporally static is such a classifier? Would a model trained on the social media posts of today work well on content created 2 years ago? Two years from now?
- Can we extend the above to make a continuous variable prediction? For example, could we predict NOMINATE scores? Could we predict ideology or partisanship generally?

- How different is the language used between elected officials in a party and voters? Could a model trained on one work effectively for others?
- Could we use a model trained on politicians with a known ideology score (e.g., NOMINATE) to predict candidates ideology before they have a voting record?
- How different is spoken text from written text from social media text? Does the modality matter?
- Clearly word order matters when communicating. What techniques could help us grapple with the dependencies between words, sentences, and paragraphs?

For more information about the topics presented in this chapter, we recommend the following resources:

- Bird, Steven, Ewan Klein, and Edward Loper. Natural language processing with Python: analyzing text with the natural language toolkit. "O'Reilly Media, Inc.", 2009.
- Manning, Christopher D., and Hinrich Schütze. Foundations of statistical natural language processing. MIT press, 1999.
- Jurafsky, Dan, and James H. Martin. Speech and language processing. Vol. 3. London:: Pearson, 2014.
- https://spacy.io/

References

1. Lewis, J. B., Poole, K., Rosenthal, H., Boche, A., Rudkin, A., & Sonnet, L. (2017). Voteview: Congressional roll-call votes database. https://voteview.com/
2. Mikolov, T., Chen, K., Corrado, G., & Dean, J. (2013). Efficient estimation of word representations in vector space. arXiv:1301.3781
3. Reese, D. (2012). Is Sen. Claire McCaskill a moderate? The Washington Post. Retrieved August 22, 2013.
4. Spärck Jones, K. (1972). A statistical interpretation of term specificity and its application in retrieval. *Journal of Documentation, 28*, 11–21.
5. van der Maaten, L., & Hinton, G. (2008). Visualizing data using t-SNE. *Journal of Machine Learning Research, 9*, 2579–2605.

Chapter 15
Conclusion

After completing the material presented in the earlier chapters of this book, you should feel comfortable writing Python programs for a variety of research purposes. This section describes the pedagogical goals of each chapter as a way to check your understanding.

The first half of the book presented skills that allow you to collect data from publicly available services to use in your own research. Chapter 1 provided a grounding in the Python programming language. Chapters 2–5 introduced fundamental concepts related to building software in any object-oriented programming language. In Chaps. 6 and 7 you learned the basics of how the Web works and how to interact with API's over the Internet using well-defined protocols (such as HTTP) and conventions (such as REST).

The second half of the book was about how to store, organize, and leverage the data that you collect. Chapters 8 and 9 showed how to store data in both SQL and NoSQL databases and presented the advantages and disadvantages of each storage mechanism depending on your use case. Chapter 10 introduced popular libraries for machine learning with Python and provided a walk-through of a basic example using a Naive Bayes classifier on textual data. Chapters 11 and 12 described two tools that we consider to be under-utilized by social scientists: linear programming for optimization problems and unit testing for validating the correctness of your code. Chapter 13 demonstrated an in-depth case study of image processing and its application to a social research question. Chapter 14 explained concepts and techniques for extracting meaning from unstructured textual data.

Both the example code shared throughout the book and the lab sessions at the end of Chaps. 2–9 are intended to show realistic examples of how to put these skills to use. By this point you should be comfortable scraping web pages and querying publicly available API's to obtain data (whether unstructured, semi-structured, or structured) to address your research questions. You also know how to persist this data in formats ranging from flat files (CSV, JSON), to in-memory stores (e.g., MongoDB), to full-fledged SQL databases. The next section suggests a few possibilities for what to do next if you are interested in learning more along these lines.

15.1 Next Steps

If you enjoyed and benefited from the topics above, where should you go from here? There are a number of strong options, and which to choose depends on your particular research plan.

For those whose primary interest is in collecting data in a tabular format to conduct analyses, both web scraping and API querying are useful. We have shown how to collect and analyze data from Twitter, Google Maps, and the U.S. Census Bureua, among others. However, this is only a small sampling of the many APIs that expose political and social data. Other examples include data.gov in the USA,[1] data.europa.eu in Europe,[2] and the United Nations' data portal.[3]

If leveraging "big data" is part of your research program, we recommend pursuing a deeper understanding of cloud computing and how to run large, distributed analyses in a cloud environment. Major cloud services include Amazon Web Services (AWS), Google Cloud Platform (GCP), and Microsoft Azure. In addition to computing resources, each of these services also has value-added offerings such as machine learning API's for data analysis. You might also consider using a containerization system such as Docker to deploy your software to these platforms. An added benefit of using Docker is that you can preserve your containers as a way of sharing your analysis in a reproducible manner. For truly large-scale analyses, look into the Apache big data ecosystem. For example, Apache Spark allows you to run your data processing code across many physical computers in a way that is easier to design and understand than traditional map-reduce jobs.

We also provided a brief introduction to machine learning in Python, but this is an area that is growing rapidly in both capabilities and popularity. The most mainstream of these frameworks is TensorFlow, originally developed by the Google Brain team and now fully open-source. TensorFlow can be used for basic analyses such as linear or logistic regression, but its real strength is neural networks for computer vision, natural language processing, and speech recognition. Keras is another popular library that provides an additional layer of abstraction on top of TensorFlow (or Torch, another machine learning framework) and allows you to get up and running quickly with advanced machine learning.

---

[1] https://www.data.gov/developers/apis.
[2] http://data.europa.eu/euodp/en/developerscorner.
[3] http://data.un.org/Host.aspx?Content=API.

15.2 Closing

It is our sincere hope that by making this material more widely available that it helps both current and future generations of social scientists to leverage the work of other communities (such as software engineering and computer science) in their research. This material is offered as another tool in your practical toolkit, in addition to other fundamental skills such as research design and statistical modeling. By learning how to collect, organize, and analyze the wide variety of data that has become available in recent years, we hope that you find both new answers and new questions that continue to move the discipline of social science forward.

Index

B
Big-O (complexity), 50

D
Dictionary, 18

E
Exceptions, 151

F
For-loop, 17

G
Git, 23
Google Maps, 95
Graph (data structure), 65

H
Hypertext Markup Language (HTML), 79

I
Image processing, 165

L
Linear programming, 143
List, 16, 60

M
Machine learning, 129

N
Natural-language-processing, 191
Neural networks, 172
NoSQL, 118

Q
Queue, 61

S
Sorting, 50
Stack, 61
Structured Query Language (SQL), 100

T
Testing (automated), 155
Tree (data structure), 63
Twitter, 91